Good Practice Guide: **Building Condition Surveys**

RIBA Good Practice Guides

Other titles in this series:

Good Practice Guide:
Building Condition Surveys

Mike Hoxley

RIBA ₩ **Publishing**

© Mike Hoxley, 2009
Published by RIBA Publishing, 15 Bonhill Street, London EC2P 2EA

ISBN 978 1 85946 308 6

Stock Code 68971

British Library Cataloguing-in-Publication Data
A catalogue record for this book is available from the British Library.

Publisher: Steven Cross
Commissioning Editor: James Thompson
Project Editor: Alasdair Deas
Designed by Ben Millbank
Typeset by Academic + Technical
Printed and bound by MPG Books, Cornwall

RIBA Publishing is part of RIBA Enterprises Ltd.
www.ribaenterprises.com

Series foreword

The *Good Practice Guide* series has been specifically developed to provide architects, and other construction professionals, with practical advice and guidance on a range of topics that affect them, and the management of their business, on a day-to-day basis.

All of the guides in the series are written in an easy-to-read, straightforward style. The guides are not meant to be definitive texts on the particular subject in question, but each guide will be the reader's first point of reference, offering them a quick overview of the key points and then providing them with a 'route map' for finding further, more detailed information. Where appropriate, checklists, tables, diagrams and case studies will be included to aid ease of use.

Good Practice Guide: Building Condition Surveys

While carrying out measured surveys of existing buildings is a core skill that all architects learn, surveying for *condition* is a skill fewer would lay claim to. Many clients require advice on the condition of their buildings not only ahead of purchase or at the beginning or end of a lease, but as a critical step prior to extension, alteration or refurbishment. As we face the challenge of retrofitting the UK's domestic housing stock for sustainability, this is an increasingly important skill for architects to add to their professional range.

Evidence from providers of professional indemnity insurance suggests that such surveys are riskier than many other activities in which architects engage. And here lies the value of this short, practical volume. It draws on a lifetime of experience in the field, and builds on the professional's existing understanding of construction technology, to point directly to the key areas which are most often missed or misunderstood in building condition surveys. From preparation for a survey, through to the causes of dampness, timber defects, inspection of services and the critical issue of creating a report, all is explained clearly and thoroughly in this valuable book.

Sunand Prasad
President, RIBA

Acknowledgements

The author gratefully acknowledges copyright permissions for the use of the following:

- Building Research Establishment, for Tables 1 and 2 of BRE Digest 251.
- CIRIA, for Figures 12 and 13 from Publication R111, *Structural Renovation of Traditional Buildings* (see www.ciriabooks.org).

About the author

Mike Hoxley is Professor of Building Surveying at Nottingham Trent University. He has been a Chartered Surveyor for over 30 years and has served as a member of the Building Surveying Professional Group Board of the RICS for several years. His PhD is from the University of Salford and his research interests include building pathology, condition inspection of buildings and the management and marketing of the professional services firm. Mike is Co-Editor of the journal *Structural Survey*.

Contents

Section 1
Introduction

In this Section:

- *Types of surveys*
- *Professional negligence*
- *Outline of the guide*

While surveying existing buildings and reporting on their condition is not the everyday work of most architects, many do carry out this type of work, either regularly or infrequently. As with any established area of work, there are expectations of what service the architect should provide to the client when inspecting and reporting on the condition of buildings, and it is the aim of this guide to outline what those expectations are. Of course, what is expected by any particular client will be influenced by whether they have commissioned this type of work before, and the courts have also provided clarity on this subject from time to time. The author is a Professor of Building Surveying and has been a chartered surveyor for over 30 years. For over half of this period he worked in private practice, where his primary activity was the assessment of condition of existing buildings. Building methods change as a result of regulation and practice, and so there is a need to keep up to date to be able to advise clients adequately. However, there is another aspect to the time dimension, and that is an awareness of the construction methods of the past. When undertaking this type of work in a particular geographical area, the surveyor needs to have knowledge of how buildings in that locality were built over the decades and centuries gone by.

In this context, the term 'surveyor' refers to any built environment professional with the capacity and inclination to *survey* property. Such professionals will include architects, surveyors, engineers and builders, and throughout this guide the term surveyor is intended to refer to any such professional carrying out a survey. In Section 4 the core knowledge that the surveyor requires is

See also: The surveyor's core knowledge, page 27

discussed. The surveyor's most important subject area is construction technology, for without this the surveyor cannot function. It is the author's very firmly and long-held conviction that elementary construction technology (i.e. domestic building technology) is by far the most important subject studied on any built environment professional degree course. In every case where the author has been called in to advise on professional negligence by a surveyor it was a failure by the surveyor to understand (or perhaps more importantly to remember) the most basic construction technology principles that was the main problem. Certainly any slips-ups the author has made have been due to this basic problem. This guide is not intended to provide this basic knowledge and it is assumed that the reader will have a sound knowledge of construction technology before considering undertaking a survey. What the guide *does* attempt to do is to point out the areas of technology that professionals most commonly ignore when carrying out surveys.

Surveys can be broadly classified into two main types:

- where *condition* is assessed, and
- where *measurements* are recorded.

The architect will be intimately acquainted with the second of these two types of activity; it is the undertaking of condition surveys that is the principal concern of this guide. Obviously it is when a home or commercial property changes ownership that there is the greatest demand for this activity. Besides transfer of ownership, the other main times when the assessment of condition is required are:

- prior to the carrying out of building or engineering works on adjacent or nearby land, and
- during or at the end of a lease to assess legal responsibility for repair (dilapidations).

Of course there may well be other occasions when the owner of a building wishes to commission an inspection for some other purpose (e.g. because they are concerned about a particular defect).

Professional negligence and professional indemnity (PI) insurance are everyday concerns of the professional workplace and no professional activity can be considered without discussing these subjects. Of all the activities undertaken by built environment professionals, the inspection of buildings is one of the

"inspection of buildings is one of the riskier types of work"

riskier types of work. In some years within recent times, insurers have paid out more in claims than they have received in premiums for survey work. In times of recession, there is frequently an increase in the incidence of claims for this area of professional activity as clients attempt to recoup from the unfortunate surveyor some of the losses they have sustained due to falling property values. In any dispute about the quality of a building survey service, a court of law and legal advisers are likely to refer to the guidance that the main professional bodies publish on this subject. The author has therefore referred throughout this guide to some of the documents published by the Royal Institution of Chartered Surveyors (RICS). In the event of a claim, it is these documents to which the courts are likely to refer – just as a court would refer to RIBA advice on building design work, were this to be carried out by, for example, a chartered building surveyor.

In Section 2 of this guide, the various types of survey are considered in greater detail. In Section 3 the preliminary steps that the surveyor needs to take before attempting to carry out the inspection are discussed. Section 4 considers the services that other consultants can provide to the surveyor and the client, while in Section 5 the equipment required to inspect buildings is outlined. The subsequent four sections are concerned with the building inspection, starting with the actual process of inspection in Section 6. Section 7 considers the essential matters that data from PI insurers suggest are the areas where most negligence claims arise. These are associated with dampness, building movement, timber defects, roof structures and coverings. Section 8 looks at the inspection of services and environmental issues, while Section 9 considers the other elements to inspect (that is, those not considered in Sections 7 and 8). Of course it is possible to carry out a first-rate inspection, but if the written report is deficient, all will have been in vain, so Section 10 considers how the report should be written. To emphasise the essentials of report writing, a case study of an actual building survey report is presented in Section 11, together with a commentary of where it could have been improved. The guide concludes with details of suggested further reading.

Section 2
Types of survey

In this Section:

- *The classification of surveys*
- *Valuation*
- *Property purchase survey and valuation*
- *Building survey*
- *Home Condition Report*
- *Other surveys*

The classification of surveys

The various types of survey undertaken by surveyors were last considered at length by the Construction Industry Council (CIC) in 1997. The CIC is a representative forum for the construction professions (including architects, engineers and surveyors) and after much discussion it produced a document entitled *Definitions of Inspections and Surveys of Buildings*. Up until that time there was some confusion over the use of terms describing the many different types of inspections it is possible to undertake. For example, a lay-person might reasonably have expected a 'structural survey' to be carried out by a structural engineer, but in fact many chartered surveyors were carrying out inspections that they described as structural surveys. This confusion was not solely in the minds of clients, as different professions were calling the same type of inspection by different names. One of the outcomes of this document was to urge members of the professional bodies not to continue to use the term 'structural survey'. In actual fact many practitioners have been slow to change and readers may be aware of cases where the old descriptions are still being used. This is partly due to the fact that other professionals (such as solicitors) who advise clients to commission surveys still use the old terms. The terms recommended by the CIC, which are used throughout this guide, are discussed below.

Domestic surveys

The vast majority of property inspections carried out in the UK are of houses, and the three main types of survey undertaken on residential property will be considered first. These are:

- the valuation
- the property purchase survey and valuation, and
- the building survey.

There have been changes in the house-selling process in England and Wales in the recent past and this has led to the possibility of a survey being commissioned by the seller. This survey, the Home Condition Report, will be discussed after consideration of the three main types of survey carried out.

Valuation

At present about seven out of ten house purchasers rely solely on the valuation carried out by their mortgage company surveyor. However, the purpose of this inspection is not to assess condition but rather to estimate values – usually the current market value and the reinstatement value for insurance purposes. Not all valuations are carried out by a surveyor acting for the mortgage company, but the inspection, research and report will follow a similar format in all cases. Where the property inspected is for rent rather than sale, the main purpose of the valuation will be to ascertain that the rental value is a true reflection of the market value.

See also: Reinstatement cost assessment for insurance, page 11

The inspection is fairly brief, and it is the research required to discover the recent selling price of similar properties in the same locality that is rather more important. Some mortgage companies insist on this comparable evidence being submitted with the mortgage valuation report. The valuation inspection will take account of relevant factors affecting value, such as condition, location and aspects of construction, that are readily observable on a walk-round inspection. The report (usually on a standard preprinted form) may be prepared by a surveyor employed directly by the mortgage company (a staff valuer) or by a panel valuer, who is a surveyor employed by a consultancy approved by the mortgage company. In

1994 the Monopolies and Mergers Commission investigated whether building societies and banks were operating in an anti-competitive manner by only allowing staff and panel valuers to act for them, but the Commission concluded that they were not. Had the Commission decided otherwise then it would have been possible for a prospective purchaser to arrange their own valuation report from an independent surveyor. It can be very difficult for consultants to be appointed to the panel of a particular mortgage lender.

The inspection of a property for a valuation should include a 'head and shoulders' viewing of the roof space, but it is not necessary to actually physically enter the roof space. Since the insurance risk is very often assessed from the results of this inspection, any significant factors affecting risk (e.g. the close proximity of trees on clay subsoils, any fire hazards and any evidence of subsidence) should be reported on.

Some lenders are moving away from the formal mortgage valuation report and are instead placing more emphasis on the ability of the borrower to repay the loan. Such companies are relying on a 'drive-past' or 'desk-top' valuation (without the surveyor inspecting the interior or any part of the property) just to ascertain whether the proposed purchase price is in the correct price bracket. This trend may well become more prevalent in the future. The valuer must not include the value of any sale inducements (such as stamp duty payments or cashback offers) when valuing new homes. The Council of Mortgage Lenders has produced a standard disclosure form that developers must complete and forward to the mortgage lender of a new home. The form is available at www.cml.org.uk/handbook.

Property purchase survey and valuation

This is an intermediate survey, between the valuation inspection described above and the building survey (discussed below), which advises on value as well as giving information on significant aspects of the condition of the dwelling. The survey is carried out under standard conditions of engagement prepared by the professional organisation of which the surveyor is a member, and the report is prepared to a standard format approved by the professional organisation. An example of this type of survey is the Homebuyer Survey and Valuation originally introduced by the Royal Institution of Chartered Surveyors in 1981 (the latest version was introduced in 2005).

This intermediate type of survey is usually described as an 'economy' service. The client accepts that not every defect will be reported on, but the surveyor is under a duty to report on the essential matters that are likely to affect the value of the property. Many more intermediate surveys than building surveys are carried out annually, but the surveyor should be aware that the level of liability is similar and so the inspection needs to be just as thorough. When carrying out the inspection the surveyor is required to carry a ladder capable of inspecting roofs 3.0 m high, but he is not expected to raise fixed floorboards or to lift fitted carpets. Those areas of the property that are accessible and which can be inspected safely should be reported on and roof spaces should be inspected. However, where the dwelling is a flat, only those roof spaces that have direct access from the flat should be inspected. The common parts (i.e. entrance hall, staircase and landing) leading to the flat should also be inspected. The services would normally be inspected and commented on, but not tested.

From January 2010, the RICS is introducing a new version of the Homebuyer

See also:
Home
Condition
Report,
page 9

Survey which has condition ratings similar to those used by the Home Condition Report described later. The new report has a 'traffic light' system of ratings: green indicates no problem; amber denotes beware; and red suggests that works are required urgently.

This economy survey is not designed for large or old dwellings or for houses requiring extensive refurbishment. For such properties, the building survey described below would be a more appropriate service for the surveyor to offer.

Building survey

The building survey is an investigation and assessment of the construction and condition of a building and does not always include advice on value. This type of survey was originally called a 'structural survey', but the CIC document referred to earlier recommends than any survey carried out by a structural engineer should be referred to as an *inspection*, *appraisal*, *investigation* or *assessment* rather than as a survey. The principal reason for this shift in thinking is that the building survey involves rather more than an investigation and assessment of the structure; it is also concerned with the fabric, finishes, grounds and services. The services would normally only be inspected, and would only be tested if the client specifically required this extension to the normal service. Of course, where the surveyor is suspicious of the condition of the services following inspection, it would be appropriate to recommend that they be tested.

The main differences between the building survey inspection and that required for the intermediate survey are that fixed floorboards should normally be raised at each floor level and secured duct covers should be opened up where this can be achieved without causing damage or without expending excessive time. Apart from these relatively minor differences, the inspection for both types of survey should be of a similar level of detail.

As a general guide, the inspection for a building survey of a three-bedroom semi-detached house would take three hours (compared with two hours for the intermediate survey and about 30 to 45 minutes for a valuation inspection). The fees, of course, vary from region to region to reflect the different property market conditions, but the fee for a building survey would be about three-times that for a valuation, with the fee for an intermediate inspection being about double that for a valuation.

Home Condition Report

Following an extensive review of the home-selling process in England and Wales, the government brought in a new system of home buying and selling in 2007. The new system requires the seller to produce a Home Information Pack (HIP) before marketing their home.

As originally envisaged, the HIP would have included a Home Condition Report (HCR) as well as legal title and search details. The HCR is similar to the inter-mediate form of survey discussed above. This element of the proposed changes sought to address a common problem with the old system: often the buyer has to renegotiate the purchase price following the receipt of the survey report. It is at this stage that many transactions stall, or even break down completely. If the buyer has read an HCR survey report before making an offer, as would be the case under the new system as originally conceived then this situation should not occur.

Unfortunately (for surveyors), the government undertook a spectacular U-turn just prior to the introduction of the system and withdrew the mandatory require-ment for the HCR to be included in the HIP. It is still possible to include an HCR, but in reality very few are prepared. Thus, one of the main benefits of the new system is no longer a legal requirement and, just as for hundreds of years, buyers continue to make offers without the benefit of explicit and professional knowledge of the condition of the home that they are hoping to acquire. There has been much speculation that HIPs will be abandoned altogether. However, the author believes that another important element of the HIP – the Energy Performance Certificate (EPC) – is so important to the government's compliance with EU Directive 2002/91/EC that HIPs are probably here to stay. The Energy Performance of Buildings Directive requires that, from January 2009, EPCs must be made available every time a building is constructed, sold or rented. The EPC is produced by an energy assessor and thus it is still necessary for every home that is about to be introduced to the market to be inspected, but it is for the purposes of the preparation of the EPC rather than for the HCR. The EPC details the current and potential energy efficiency of the dwelling and any professional wishing to produce these must qualify as a Domestic Energy Assessor. Similarly, any surveyor wishing to prepare HCRs must first qualify as a Home Inspector. The HCR requires the Home Inspector to rate the condition of the various elements of the building using a four-point scale. For a sample HCR, see www.homeinformationpacks.gov.uk/pdf/sampleHCR.pdf.

Other surveys

The other types of inspection described in the CIC definitions document are now considered briefly.

Elemental or specialist investigation

This will be required where concern exists over specific parts of, or defects in, a building. Examples of this specialist work are a detailed study of movement, cracking, bulging, timber decay or dampness, or the testing of the electrical wiring. Such an inspection may arise as a result of one of the inspections already discussed, where the surveyor has recommended that further investigation is necessary. The scope of this type of investigation will be specific to each individual job and may involve an inspection by one or more professionals and possibly the input from trade specialists.

Investigation prior to alteration

This may be required prior to the extension or alteration of an existing building. Subject to the necessary authority being obtained from the building owner, it may involve opening up, measuring, calculations to check the adequacy of structural and service elements and detailed tests. This investigation can be more detailed than that required for a building survey and is likely to involve the services of a number of specialists.

Reinstatement cost assessment for insurance

This service is very often carried out as part of the four domestic surveys described above, but it can of course be provided independently. It will also be carried out for commercial buildings. It involves the measurement of the gross external floor area of the building and the application of an appropriate unit rate (usually £ per square metre) in order to estimate the cost of demolition and reconstruction, including all fees. This cost will have no direct relationship to the market value of the property, and indeed for a large building located in a modestly priced area can be several times greater than the market value. Usually, a reinstatement cost assessment will be made by reference to figures published by the Royal Institution of Chartered Surveyors/Building Cost Information Service (RICS/BCIS). However, the Association of British Insurers also produces useful summary tables of unit rates for domestic properties, which are available online. Where the building is non-standard or has particularly valuable features (e.g. where the building is listed), it may only be possible to assess reconstruction costs by preparing and costing approximate building quantities. Obviously, in such instances the fee quoted for this service would need to reflect the work required.

Stock condition survey

This will be commissioned to assess the state of repair or condition of an organisation's current building stock in connection with the preparation of a planned preventative maintenance programme. Perhaps the most common client for such a service would be an affordable-housing landlord, but any owner of a large number of buildings could commission this service. Most large property owners maintain quite sophisticated computerised databases of their portfolios, and surveyors carrying out stock condition inspections are often required to enter data directly into hand-held computers on site.

Schedule of condition

This records the condition of a building at a particular point in time. The report, which is often supported by photographs, sketches and drawings, should be in sufficient detail so that any subsequent defects or items of disrepair can be readily identified. The two most common situations that require the preparation of schedules of condition are at the start of a lease and prior to the commencement of adjacent construction or engineering work. In the first instance, it is usual for the tenant (who will be responsible for the upkeep of the building) to want to have a record of the building's condition when their liability commenced. In the second scenario, the owner of the property may wish to make a claim if any damage arises from the building or engineering works and will therefore need to have an agreed record of the property's condition before any work commences. It is usual for a schedule of condition to have a tabular format, and in some respects the preparation of such a schedule is less onerous than, for example, the carrying out of a building survey. If defects are present, it is sufficient to merely record the precise extent of these (e.g. by sketching any cracks to show their width and length) rather than to analyse why the defects have occurred.

Schedule of dilapidations

A schedule of dilapidations is required to identify any items of disrepair in a tenanted property under the terms of a lease. It may be prepared for service on the landlord or the tenant, depending on their respective obligations for repairs under the lease. A schedule may be terminal (served at the end of the lease) or interim (served where the lease has three or more years to run). The purpose of the interim schedule is to point out the repairs that the tenant is required to carry out to fulfil the obligations under the lease. It is usually far less detailed than a terminal schedule. Both types of schedule are usually produced in tabular form, and in the later stages of the process the schedule will need to be priced to quantify the dilapidations. It is usual for both the tenant and the landlord to appoint a surveyor and for the surveyors to agree the extent and cost of work required. Where agreement cannot be reached then the matter will proceed to litigation; in such instances a Scott schedule will be produced. The Scott schedule summarises the position of both parties over each alleged item of disrepair and is used by the court to cost the final settlement.

Measured survey

A measured (or dimensional survey) involves taking measurements of a building and/or site in order to prepare accurate drawings to scale, usually prior to the design of alteration or extension works. Such a survey may include taking levels.

Inspection of buildings under construction

The final type of inspection defined by the CIC is the inspection of buildings under construction. Such inspections are required for a variety of reasons and the exact purpose will dictate the frequency and scope of the inspection and the reporting format. Examples of this type of inspection are the statutory inspections required under the Building Regulations and certification inspections required under building contracts. A particularly common service that falls under this category is the inspection to certify the construction of a new dwelling. Inspections of this type may be carried out by an employee of the National House Building Council or a similar scheme or by an independent architect or surveyor. Certification that the construction of a house is satisfactory is usually a prerequisite of obtaining mortgage funding to purchase a new house. In this case, the surveyor makes approximately ten inspections at predetermined stages (from the inspection of the foundation trenches through to completion) and certifies that the work is in accordance with the approved drawings and that it complies with good practice.

A number of other types of survey are not specifically mentioned in the CIC document, and these are considered below.

Commercial properties

Most of the inspections described above are equally applicable to commercial property as they are to residential buildings. The exceptions are the property purchase survey and valuation (which was specifically introduced for modestly sized domestic property) and the HCR. The estimation of rental values for commercial property is also a specialist activity and is usually carried out by a valuation surveyor.

The commercial building surveyor requires an awareness of a broader range of legislation than does a surveyor who inspects only domestic property. A working knowledge of the legislation relating to fire precautions and health and safety, for example, is required.

Furthermore, the potential costs of professional negligence can be very much higher for commercial property than for residential buildings. This is because any consequent loss claims could be so much greater. If, for example, a surveyor failed to notice roof defects in a warehouse where expensive goods were being stored, the costs of replacing the damaged goods could be very much higher than the cost of re-roofing the building.

See also:
Professional
indemnity
insurance,
page 20

Ecclesiastical inspections

The survey of churches is a specialist activity, and indeed some architects and surveyors specialise in this work to the exclusion of all other professional activities. The Church of England's maintenance programme is formalised and has as its basis a quinquennial review of all churches: church buildings are inspected every five years and a programme of maintenance, repair and improvement works is drawn up for the period up to the next review. Other denominations, such as Roman Catholics and Methodists, often have a similar regular inspection programme. In this sense, this type of inspection could come under the earlier heading of stock condition survey. However, the stock is rather specialised and traditionally the architect or surveyor responsible for a particular church has maintained a long-term relationship with the building.

Historic buildings

Just as some professionals specialise in ecclesiastical work so others confine their activities to historic buildings. The conservation profession has become increasingly important in the past decade or so and many architects, engineers and surveyors specialise in this form of work. The Society for the Protection of Ancient Buildings (SPAB) has been at the forefront of a rethink on how to conserve our built heritage and offers advice on both the principles and practice of conservation to professionals and building owners. SPAB is particularly keen to promote detailed consideration by prospective purchasers of historic buildings. Its 'look before you leap' campaign has stressed the importance of clients taking professional advice before they purchase, so that they do not do irreversible damage to the building in their haste to adapt it to their needs. Rather, SPAB advocates that historic property owners should adapt themselves to the existing building, instead of the other way round. SPAB's website (www.spab.org.uk) offers advice to clients wishing to instruct a surveyor of a historic building.

S U M M A R Y

- Before the CIC provided clarity on this subject there was much confusion in the minds of clients, and sometimes in the minds of their professional advisers, over the titles given to the various types of survey.
- You should still be aware, however, that many members of the public and professionals (principally solicitors and estate agents) will still use the term 'structural survey' when they mean 'building survey'.
- The three most common inspections of residential property are the valuation, the intermediate property purchase survey and valuation and the building survey.
- The intermediate survey also forms the basis of the Home Condition Report (HCR), which is a seller-commissioned report that can be included in a HIP in England and Wales but which is not commonly provided.
- The qualification of Home Inspector is required by those carrying out HCRs.
- A schedule of condition is usually required by a tenant entering into a lease that imposes repairing obligations on them, or prior to large building or engineering works on adjoining land (including works which come under the remit of the Party Wall etc. Act 1996).
- A schedule of dilapidations is required during, or at the end of, a lease to ascertain whether the tenant is fulfilling, or has fulfilled, their repairing obligations.
- Inspections of historic building, and in particular churches, are undertaken by professionals who specialise in this type of work (including many architects).

Section 3
Getting ready to survey

In this Section:

- *Taking instructions*
- *Conditions of engagement*
- *Fees*
- *Professional indemnity insurance*
- *Visit to site*
- *Initial research*
- *Surveying safely*

Introduction

This section is concerned with the essential matters that the surveyor needs to attend to before leaving the office to carry out a survey. Professional indemnity insurers advise that there are more problems with this aspect of surveying work than any other. It is simply not possible to rush off and carry out a survey immediately on receiving a telephone instruction to do so – there are a number of preliminary steps that are required to clarify exactly what the client requires and how the service will be provided. If nothing else, a number of legal niceties must be attended to before the survey is undertaken. This section also considers the sources of information that the surveyor is likely to rely on – other than that yielded by the inspection itself.

Taking instructions

As implied by the comment above, many commissions initially come via the telephone, but it is not always the client at the other end of the line. It may be that a solicitor or licensed conveyancer contacts the surveyor to arrange the survey. Other professionals who may recommend or refer clients to surveyors are estate agents, accountants, bank managers and building society managers. The surveyor must ensure, however, that the instructions are taken directly from the client, which will mean obtaining the client's contact details from the referrer so that they can be approached directly.

The first thing to be ascertained is which of the wide variety of surveys described in Section 2 the client requires. Let us assume for the purpose of this discussion that the client requires a building survey of a residential property and that the surveyor has telephoned the client in response to a referral from the client's solicitor. The surveyor should ascertain basic details of the property:

• type (house or flat)
• whether detached, semi-detached or terraced
• approximate age
• size (number of storeys, number of rooms), and
• location.

This information should enable the surveyor to quote a fee, which is what the client will be particularly interested in. The surveyor should offer preliminary advice as to the suitability of the type of survey required. For example, if the client were to request a Homebuyer Survey of a large, old or dilapidated dwelling, the surveyor would have to advise that such a service would be inappropriate.

The client may require the services of other specialists, such as an electrician or a timber and damp-proofing contractor, and the surveyor should indicate the availability, suitability and likely cost of such inspections. Once the client has agreed to pay the amount quoted by the surveyor, it is necessary to send the client the conditions of engagement and for the client to agree the conditions.

See also: Section 4, Help from specialists, page 27

Conditions of engagement

There have been instances where clients have successfully sued surveyors on the basis that they were expecting a full building survey but the surveyor has only provided an inspection and valuation. In order to avoid this possible problem, precise details of the service to be provided must be agreed in writing by both parties before the survey is undertaken – this is the main reason why a survey cannot be carried out immediately on receipt of instructions. In the scenario outlined above, the surveyor would deliver or post written conditions of engagement to the client. Most surveyors have standard conditions, and indeed if a Homebuyer Survey is to be provided then the standard RICS conditions of engagement would be used. It is important for conditions

"precise details of the service to be provided must be agreed"

of engagement to spell out in great detail what will be undertaken during the inspection and reporting stages of the survey, and perhaps more importantly what will *not* be provided.

It may be sufficient for the surveyor merely to notify the conditions of engagement to the client. However, to avoid any ambiguity later, it is much better to have some mechanism for the client to agree in writing that they have read the conditions and agree to them. Again, most firms have a standard form which the client signs and returns to the surveyor. Once the surveyor has received the signed form it is safe for the surveyor to carry out the survey.

Which? (formerly known as The Consumers' Association) has been very critical of some surveyors' written conditions of engagement, in that it believes they are overly long and over-complicated. Indeed, it was criticism from Which? that prompted the RICS to reduce significantly the length and complexity of the standard conditions of engagement for the Homebuyer Survey and Valuation. Most surveyors would be well advised to follow the example of the RICS in this regard.

Fees

Since the professional bodies representing property and construction professionals abolished mandatory fee scales in the 1980s it is no longer possible for the RIBA or the RICS to publish fee scales. Indeed, the Office of Fair Trading has also outlawed *recommended* fee scales for such services. It is, of course, local competition that determines the levels of survey fees in any particular locality. If in doubt as to what the market will bear, it is probably best to telephone a few surveyors in the guise of a potential client and to be quoted fees for carrying out various types of survey.

When a mortgage applicant instructs a building society or bank valuer it is usual for the fee to be collected in advance. As a result of this practice, many surveyors have adopted similar arrangements for the collection of survey fees prior to undertaking the survey. Solicitors and estate agents, two of the other professionals involved in the house buying and selling process, have adopted procedures that ensure they collect payment of their fees before the legal transaction is completed. It is not surprising, therefore, that most surveyors attempt to ensure that there is some certainty of them receiving payment. At one time, the author practised in an area of the UK that is popular with holiday-makers and where property values were relatively low. It was quite common for holidaymakers to fall in love with the area during a summer visit and to decide to purchase a second home. If the fee was not collected in advance then it was sometimes difficult to obtain payment as some clients would rapidly go off the idea of purchasing the property once they had returned home.

Professional indemnity insurance

Evidence from professional indemnity (PI) insurers suggests that survey and valuation work is one of the highest risk activities undertaken by property and construction professionals. Over the past 30 years or so, the incidence and value of claims have been substantially higher than for other property activities, such as estate agency and architecture. Of course, if a client purchases a property that contains defects of which they were not aware after reading a survey report, it is only natural that the client will seek financial recompense from the surveyor. It is therefore essential that the surveyor report all *relevant* defects. What is considered relevant in any given situation will depend on the type of survey carried out.

In an increasingly litigious and consumer-orientated society, the definition of what constitutes professional negligence seems to have narrowed in the popular mind to that of making any mistake whatsoever. The legal liability that any professional incurs in carrying out a professional service for a client stems from common law, in particular the tort of negligence. The professional's primary responsibility is to perform the service with reasonable skill and care. Failure to meet this standard, by omission or act, is likely to be deemed professional negligence.

For a claim to succeed in negligence there must be a breach of a duty of care and damage must result from the breach. Very often, the only defence a professional has against a claim of negligence is that the subject dealt with is not generally known to the profession – called the 'state of art' defence.

The professional institutions are anxious that their members' clients are not disadvantaged by the negligent acts of their members and so many have a system of compulsory PI insurance. Some (e.g. the Law Society) act as the insurer of last resort for its members. The RIBA and the Architects Registration Board (ARB) require all RIBA firms and all registered architects to be covered by a PI insurance policy. RIBA Insurance Agency is the only broker endorsed by the RIBA to provide PI insurance to its members, although members are free to obtain cover elsewhere. Any architect undertaking building condition surveys should ensure that their policy provides appropriate cover, but in view of the foregoing discussion, they should be aware that cover for this type of activity might be more expensive than for other professional activities.

PI insurance is offered on a 'claims made' basis. This means that it is necessary for the surveyor to have insurance *at the time that a claim is made.* Therefore, it is necessary for surveyors to maintain 'run-off cover' after they have retired. The minimum duration of such cover required by the ARB is six years. RIBA Guidance Note 5, however, recommends that a much longer period be adopted: a claim can be brought up to six years after the discovery of a defect (and 12 years when a contract is under deed) and up to 15 years later for a negligence claim in tort.

Many construction professionals find PI insurance to be prohibitively expensive. Furthermore, because the uninsured excesses for certain types of work are so high, a successful claim by a client can severely affect the financial standing of a professional. It is not uncommon for a surveyor to have to find the first £5,000 or £10,000 of any claim from their own pocket.

The considerable increase in the incidence of PI claims means it is likely that a surveyor will have at least one claim made against them during their career. It is very important therefore to be aware of the correct procedure to follow in the unfortunate event of a claim

"a surveyor will have at least one claim made against them during their career"

being made. Of course, each insurance policy will be slightly different, so the surveyor should check their policy before taking any action, but the following general comments are offered for guidance.

Most policies require the insurer to be notified in the event of a claim arising. Thus even if the surveyor believes that the value of a claim is likely to fall within the uninsured excess, it is still necessary to notify the insurer. The reason for this is that small claims often have the nasty habit of developing into bigger claims – particularly when the lawyers get involved! Most policies stipulate that the insured should never admit liability, even if they believe that they have been negligent. Being accused of negligence can of course be a traumatic experience, and so it is always better for another surveyor in the firm to deal with the complaint. Of course, where the surveyor is a sole principal this will not be possible.

If the surveyor is unfortunate enough to face a claim that proceeds to court then it is the insurer who will decide when or if the claim should be settled. Thus, a surveyor may believe that they have not been negligent, but the insurer, wary of incurring the enormous costs that a court case will entail, may insist on settling – even though this means the poor surveyor is then liable for the uninsured excess. This can be overcome to some extent by having a 'QC' clause in the PI policy.

The subjects of professional negligence and PI insurance are by their very nature rather depressing. However, the wise surveyor will ensure that they are at the forefront of their mind when carrying out any service for a client – particularly during the risky business of a building or other survey.

Visit to site

When quoting a fee for the survey of an unusual property, the surveyor may decide that they cannot do this without first visiting the site. This is an eminently sensible idea as it is obviously far better to discover something likely to affect the cost of providing the service before a fee has been quoted rather than after. Provided that the property is within reasonable travelling distance of the surveyor's office, a preliminary visit to site is always a good idea, even where the conditions of engagement have been finalised. The initial 15–30 minutes on site when carrying out a survey are very often spent familiarising oneself with the layout of the site and buildings. An initial visit prepares the surveyor in advance, reducing this familiarisation time. It will also help the surveyor to identify whether specialist equipment or consultants will be required to carry out the inspection.

Initial research

For a building of non-straightforward construction, a preliminary visit may well inform the surveyor that it would be an advantage to obtain the original or as-built drawings. It is not always possible to determine exact details of construction without some drawings to assist, particularly in a commercial building. Of course the usual rider needs to be added here, that the building may not have been constructed exactly as originally designed. The author is aware of cases where even drawings marked as 'as built' differ significantly in some detail from what was actually constructed on site. Nevertheless, drawings can sometimes be a useful source of information. A visit to the local authority building control office can often prove fruitful in this respect. Even if the drawings cannot be inspected in great detail in the council offices, it will usually be possible to discover who the original architect was. It will normally be possible to obtain copies of the drawings from the original architect – provided of course that the building is reasonably modern. Other sources of information the surveyor may consult are considered below.

The vast majority of information that the surveyor needs to process before writing the report will result from their physical inspection of the building. However, the surveyor will undoubtedly also obtain information from third parties, and it is necessary to consider how credible these additional sources of information are. If, for example, the surveyor is told that a flat roof, to which access is particularly difficult, has been re-covered within the past 12 months, what should they do? Should the surveyor believe that source, or arrange for a longer ladder to inspect the roof? The answer to this question depends in part on just who the source of information is. If the source is the owner, who obviously has a considerable vested interest, then the surveyor should treat the information with suspicion; if, however, the source is a local authority officer then it is more likely that the information can be relied on. Of course, there is no better source than the evidence of one's own eyes, and if it is not

"there is no better source than the evidence of one's own eyes"

too much trouble to get a longer ladder then this is what should be done. In the vast majority of cases the need for additional information will only become apparent after the inspection has been carried out, but it is possible that the information will be sought either before or after the inspection. Possible sources of information are considered below.

Existing owner

As indicated above, anyone who has a vested interest in the disposal of a property should not be treated as a credible source of information. This obviously includes the existing owner of the property and the estate agent acting on their behalf. However, the owner of the property (or the estate agent) is likely to be the one person with whom the surveyor comes into contact. Information provided by the owner should, wherever possible, be verified by a third person. Where it is not possible to do this then the surveyor's report should clearly state that the evidence has been provided by the owner or the estate agent but that the surveyor is not able to confirm this information. Where the information is of a legal nature then of course the client should be advised to consult a solicitor or conveyancer. One fact that owners of property are prone to exaggerate is the size of their plot.

Solicitor

By and large one can assume that information provided by a solicitor or conveyancer is reliable. When inspecting leased property it is essential that the surveyor is familiar with the contents of the lease, in so far as repairing obligations are concerned. The client should always be referred to the solicitor if there are any issues regarding the liability for the repair of boundary walls and fences. The deeds will usually make reference to these and information provided by owners, and in particular by neighbours, in this regard is often far from reliable.

Local authority

Valuable information about planning matters and hidden construction details can often be obtained from the relevant local authority department. Access to the original planning or Building Regulations drawings will often be provided by local authority officers. It may also be possible to approach the original architect to obtain copies of these drawings. Of course, the problem with relying on original drawings is that the building may not have been constructed as designed, but provided the building is not too old then the original architect may well be able to provide important information – either from contemporary records or from memory.

With old buildings, particularly those which are listed or located in a conservation area, the local authority conservation officer is often a very valuable source of information. Most conservation officers are particularly enthusiastic about the buildings under their care and are only too happy to provide any information that they possess. The local historical society could also be consulted when any specific details are required. There may also be a local archive of film and photographic images, which could provide specific information about the past façade of a particular building. Such detailed information may take some time to trace and its sourcing will often be beyond the scope of an initial purchase inspection. The information may, however, be useful for any follow-on design commission.

Other parties

The RICS Guidance Note *Building Surveys of Residential Property* (RICS, 2004a, p. 12) points out that:

> Information may be available from the property owner, occupier or, where the property is vacant, the owner's agent about matters affecting the property. It is advised that this is used as a guide. However, it is worth remembering that information supplied may not be entirely accurate, but the primary purpose of this procedure is to assist the surveyor in establishing matters of relevance and to follow a trail of prudent enquiry.

Sometimes, the surveyor will discover that this information is volunteered by complete strangers. Many neighbours are seemingly very keen to impart information about previous underpinning or Second World War bomb damage, and so on. As the RICS Guidance Note suggests, this information can very often prove useful, more often than not as a primer for discovering more detailed information. One should, of course, be very wary about accepting the word of a complete stranger without obtaining any corroborating evidence.

Surveying safely

In preparing for a survey it is necessary to consider the safety of all personnel involved in the exercise. Advice about the safe use of surveying equipment and other safety matters is contained in RICS (2004b).

SUMMARY

- A number of essential activities must be undertaken before carrying out a survey.
- Detailed instructions must be obtained and these should be confirmed in writing, preferably with the client's written acceptance.
- Many surveyors take this opportunity to obtain advance payment of their fees.
- It is essential that PI insurance is in place – statistics from insurers suggest surveying is a riskier service than general architectural work or estate agency.
- Information may be available from the property owner, occupier or, where the property is vacant, the owner's agent about matters affecting the property. It is advised that this is used as a guide only.
- Provided it is practical, a preliminary site visit can save time during the early part of the actual survey and can inform the surveyor what initial research is required and what specialist equipment and consultants may be needed.

Section 4
Help from specialists

In this Section:

- *The surveyor's core knowledge*
- *Other professionals*
- *Contractors*
- *Engagement of specialists*
- *Which specialists are being used?*

The surveyor's core knowledge

It is one of the essential characteristics of a professional that they are aware of the boundaries of their own competence and that they know when to seek advice from, or to refer their client to, a specialist. General practice doctors refer patients to specialists when confronted with acute symptoms they are not sure of, solicitors refer clients to the appropriate barrister, and so on. As the world becomes more and more complicated, it is impossible for any practitioner in any professional field to have all the knowledge and experience to be able to advise every client about every problem in a particular field of expertise.

This discussion leads us to ask the question 'what is the professional's core knowledge?'. Certainly in the case of the medical GP there is widespread understanding of what that core knowledge is – a general knowledge of anatomy and physiology and an ability to diagnose the symptoms with which a patient presents. When one asks the same question about a surveyor the answer depends on what type of surveyor we are considering. A valuation surveyor's core knowledge is an a-wareness of local property markets – be they residential or commercial. On the other hand, a surveyor who is principally concerned with assessing condition requires other knowledge, in particular a thorough understanding of construction technology. Unless they are completely aware of how the building being inspected has been (or, perhaps more importantly, should have been) constructed, the surveyor will not be in a position to detect defects.

Of course this knowledge also has a time dimension, in that the building being inspected may have been erected at any time over the past thousand years. Not all surveyors would feel confident inspecting a very old building, and in such situations the surveyor would no doubt refer the client to a surveyor who specialises in historic buildings. The age of the properties a surveyor is likely to inspect will obviously depend on the location in which they practice. A surveyor working in the centre of, say, Oxford is likely to inspect many more older buildings than a surveyor practising in Milton Keynes.

This introduces the question of the size of the geographical area over which a particular surveyor should be prepared to undertake inspections. There are certain building types that are peculiar to a particular region. Clay lump is largely limited to areas of East Anglia (although earth buildings have different names in other parts of the UK). Early timber-framed buildings are constructed in different ways in different parts of the country. Building terminology also varies from region to region. If a surveyor is to have an awareness of the geology and how this impacts on the potential for foundation failure in a particular locality, it is likely that the surveyor will restrict themselves to working within a fairly limited geographical area. Of course the density of development also needs to be considered in this context. A surveyor may well be able to make a living by operating exclusively in a particular urban location, whereas a surveyor working in a rural setting will have to travel much further in order to operate in an economically sustainable manner.

So far then we have said that the surveyor needs to have knowledge of building construction and that this knowledge should be in the context of the particular locality in which they accept instructions. Other essential requirements are an awareness of:

- how buildings fail
- how buildings deteriorate over time, and
- how buildings can be returned to satisfactory condition after they have failed or deteriorated.

For a simple domestic building situated within the locality in which an experienced surveyor works, it is possible that the surveyor will possess the entire knowledge necessary to carry out a complete and thorough survey of the property. Such instances will be in the minority. In most situations it will be necessary to call on the services of specialists if a complete service is to be provided to the client. Very often it is for the surveyor concerned to make the decision about when it is necessary to refer to or call on a specialist. Failure in this respect could have dire consequences. The employment of specialists needs to be considered both at the time of accepting instructions and when reporting to the client. However, before discussing this aspect, the various types of specialist who may be employed will be considered.

Other professionals

The specialists likely to be called in to assist the surveyor will either be fellow professionals or contractors or tradespeople. The first of the other consultants likely to be involved is the structural engineer. The client is paying for a 'survey' and will be less than impressed if the surveyor employs another consultant to advise on simple movement of a traditional building, such as settlement or subsidence. The diagnosis and rectification of such defects is part of the surveyor's core knowledge referred to above. However, there will undoubtedly be instances where the structural engineer's expertise is required. An example is where a chimney breast has been removed within a building but remains within a roof space. In many such situations it is possible to say that the method of support is inadequate (e.g. where the support is off a slender ceiling joist). In others situations, however, the decision is more finely balanced; for example, where a large-section timber has been used. Some surveyors would be confident in checking by calculation whether the particular section used was adequate; others, however, would prefer to call on the services of a structural engineer to verify the method of support. Other situations that may demand the services of a structural engineer include excessive deflection of components that needs to be checked by calculation or where specialised foundations are involved.

An acoustics engineer may be required where there is doubt about the soundproofing of a separating or party wall, or where the acoustic performance of special spaces, such as an auditorium or meeting hall, requires assessing. Such services are only likely to be required in exceptional circumstances, and then only for commercial buildings. For specialist sanitary and drainage installations of commercial buildings it is possible that the services of a civil engineer will be required, but in smaller domestic-scale buildings it is more likely that a general builder or specialist tradesperson will be employed to undertake drainage inspections and tests. Similarly, in a particularly complicated commercial building it is likely that building services engineers will be employed to inspect and report on the service installations. For a dwelling, however, a heating engineer or plumber may be engaged to survey the heating and domestic hot and cold water installations. Where a specialist is not employed then the surveyor would be expected to report on the type, age and condition of the plumbing installations.

Contractors

There are occasions when it is impossible to determine the full extent of a method of construction or defect without opening up of the structure. Provided that the owner of the property is willing for such opening up to take place, it is likely that the surveyor will wish to engage a general building contractor to undertake the necessary opening up and, if necessary, the subsequent reinstatement work. There will no doubt be some survey work, particularly where large-scale refurbishment or alteration is planned, where the work carried out by a general contractor is extensive. Conversely, it is unlikely that the seller of a pristine dwelling would be willing to allow for any opening up whatsoever.

When inspecting drainage installations the surveyor is expected to locate and identify inspection chambers and also to raise the covers to determine the likelihood of any problems. The presence of blockages and tree roots will obviously give cause for concern, and the condition of the inspection chambers is a guide to the general condition of the installation. Raising corroded iron or steel covers can be difficult and the surveyor will need to carry a variety of implements for carrying out this task. There may be occasions when the surveyor will need to engage a contractor to lift a particularly tightly fitting cover, and in some extreme situations it may be necessary to break and replace a cover.

See also: Section 5, The tools of the surveyor, page 37

In some situations a general contractor may be the most appropriate person to undertake drain testing, but there are specialist contractors who may be able to undertake this work more competitively. Drain runs have traditionally been pressure tested by filling them with water or air. Smoke testing is appropriate for drains above ground, and the use of dyes enables drain runs to be traced.

Of course new drains are always subjected to a water pressure test as part of the Building Regulations compliance process. However, pressure tests can damage old drains, particularly those with weak joints, and the permission of the owner of the property should always be obtained before applying a water or air test to any drain. Some surveyors carry their own drain testing equipment with them and are prepared to apply their own tests. However, this is only really appropriate for drainage layouts of limited size. Where the installation is extensive it would take several hours to apply water or air tests and this is hardly the most economical use of the surveyor's time.

> *See also: Section 5, The tools of the surveyor, page 37*

Applying a pressure test to a drain run will reveal whether or not the drain is watertight, but it will not identify where the leak is occurring. This fact together with the risk of damage to existing drains is the main reason why pressure testing is increasingly being replaced by CCTV surveys, in which a specialist contractor uses specially adapted drain rods to run a small video camera along the full length of a drain. The survey consists of a video that will identify exactly where a defect is located. The only disadvantage of a video inspection is that the extent of any leakage is not revealed. As a result of increasing competition, the costs of video surveys of drainage installations have fallen significantly since they were first introduced.

The electrical installation of a building is another area where the surveyor may require specialist advice. As discussed in Section 8, as a minimum it is necessary for the surveyor to identify:

> *See also: Electrical installations, page 76*

• type of mains supply
• location and type of meters and consumer units, and
• type and approximate age of the wiring and fittings.

Earthing arrangements may also need to be commented on.

Where it is obvious from the age of the wiring and fittings that extensive rewiring works are necessary it is of course appropriate for the surveyor to advise that this is the case and recommend that competitive quotations are obtained. There is rather more of a problem when the installation appears to have modern wiring and fittings – how far should the surveyor inspect in this situation? What is required of the surveyor is an *inspection* – at present there is no require-ment for the surveyor to *test* the installation (however, this situation may change in the foreseeable future). The IEE Wiring Regulations do not have the same statutory force as, say, the Building Regulations, but the mains service provider will normally require certification that a new installation complies with the IEE Regulations (BSI, 2008) before connecting the property to the mains supply. The IEE Regulations also state that an installation should be tested every five years. It would therefore be appropriate in the circumstances suggested above to recommend to a purchaser that a copy of the latest certificate be obtained. Of course where a client specifically requests that an electrical test is carried out then the surveyor is able to pass on their liability in respect of the electrical installation to the electrician engaged to provide this service.

At the heart of the core knowledge expected of the surveyor is the ability to detect, categorise and recommend remedial work for damp problems and fungal attack and insect infestation in timber. As a general rule, therefore, specialist advice should only be sought in connection with the likely cost of remedial works. It must always be remembered that specialist damp and timber treatment companies are in business to sell their remedial work. While some of these firms are reputable, many are not – as evidenced by several high-profile cases reported in the media recently. There are very few damp and timber treatment consultants who only exist to offer advice, and such consultants would of course charge fees for such advice.

The difficulty with dampness problem diagnosis is that it is not always easy to distinguish accurately between penetrating or rising dampness and condensation. Quite detailed environmental monitoring of internal ambient temperature and absolute and relative humidity is sometimes necessary over several weeks, or even months, to be absolutely certain as to the cause of some dampness problems. Obviously, such monitoring is beyond the scope of most surveys, but it would be appropriate for the surveyor to recommend such testing where they are not able to diagnose a particular dampness problem from a simple visual inspection and the use of a moisture meter. Similarly, it is not always easy to distinguish between dry rot and wet rot, although of course dry rot remedial works are very much more expensive. Accurate diagnosis is therefore of considerable importance, and this may involve some opening up of the structure to search for the telltale signs of dry rot. The surveyor is expected to identify whether any insect

"where estimates are sought for clients, more than one estimate should be obtained"

infestation is active or not, and to distinguish between the various types of insect, but a specialist contractor should be consulted regarding the estimated cost of remedial work. As with all cases where estimates are sought for clients, more than one estimate should be obtained.

See also: Fungal attack, page 68

Engagement of specialists

The appointment of specialists should first be considered at the time when instructions are taken from the client. It may be that the client has quite firm ideas about the level of service they require and might request that drainage and electrical tests be included from the beginning. In other situations, the surveyor may recommend the appointment of a particular specialist after discussing the matter with the client over the telephone. For example, where the surveyor is aware that most properties in a particular location have pitch fibre drains it is likely that a specialist drainage survey will be recommended from the outset. In such situations it is always best for the client to appoint the specialist contractor or consultant directly. Such an arrangement has two advantages:

- the specialist will be responsible for collecting their fee directly from the client
- if there is any subsequent dispute between the parties, the surveyor does not need to become involved.

Of course, in many situations the surveyor will not know that a specialist is required until the inspection has actually been carried out. In such situations, it would be appropriate for the surveyor to recommend in their report that the client engages the services of the specialist. However, it is always best to advise the client of the need for a specialist at the earliest opportunity. A client is unlikely to be impressed if, after waiting some time for a survey report to arrive, they discover that it is merely a list of specialists to be consulted. In fact it was precisely this issue that concerned Which? and which persuaded the RICS to revise its Homebuyer Survey in 1998 (although some commentators believe that the changes introduced have made little improvement in this regard). A surveyor must not merely hide behind the skirts of a string of specialists they recommend to inspect the property, but must give their own professional opinion wherever possible. The surveyor has to balance the need not to overstep the boundaries of their own competence with the need to provide what the client is actually paying for – a professional opinion. The surveyor can, by all means, recommend that specialists provide estimates of the cost of remedial work, but they must not recommend that others provide the actual service that the client expects from them.

Which specialists are being used?

Readers may be interested to see exactly what type of work is being referred to specialists by surveyors. An indication of this is given in Table 4.1, which shows the percentages of a sample of UK building surveyors who refer the use of surveying equipment to specialist contractors or consultants. (The research project is described in more detail in Section 5.)

See also:
Investigating practice, page 40

The results shown in Table 4.1 are fairly predictable in that the tasks most commonly referred are the use of an endoscope, electrical and drain testing, chemical analysis of concrete and mortar and the use of a reinforcement cover meter. About one-fifth of the surveyors in the sample also refer flat-roof leak detection and electronic paint-gauge measurement. There appears to be a slight trend towards following the US practice of the surveyor taking on more responsibility for testing services, but the results of this research confirm the traditional view that electrical and drain testing is currently the work most often referred to specialists.

Now that the surveyor has agreed the conditions of engagement with the client and which specialists will be used to assist in the survey, it is nearly time to leave the office to undertake the inspection!

TABLE 4.1: *Percentages of surveyors referring use of equipment*

Equipment	Percentage referring (n = 143)	Equipment	Percentage referring (n = 143)
Recording/viewing		Environmental	
thermal image camera	11.9	moisture meter: pin probe	3.5
digital camera	0.7	moisture meter: surface	1.4
video camera	1.4	moisture meter: other	9.1
35mm camera	0.7	Material detectors	
endoscope	25.9	Studmaster	5.6
hand lens	0	metal detector	7.7
binoculars	0	Electrical testing	
inspection mirror	0	earth meter	37.8
compass	0	mains tester	37.1
battery torch	0	other tester	14.0
electric survey lighting	0.7	Drain testing	
Dictaphone	0	CCTV	60.8
microscope	7.0	smoke bomb	32.9
image analysis software	3.5	fluid dye	31.5
PC with word processor or spreadsheet	0.7	bung/balloon stopper	32.9
PC with diagnosis software	0.7	Metals	
Measurement		electronic paint gauge	19.6
steel tape	0	Timber	
fabric tape	0	integrity awl	6.3
electronic measure	0.7	Sibert integrity drill	7.7
tread-wheel	4.9	Concrete/mortar	
crack width measurer	3.5	chemical analysis kit	32.9
movement measurer	8.4	ISAT permeability	13.3
level	10.5	rebound hammer	19.6
plumb line etc.	2.1	reinforcement cover meter	25.2
Environmental		radar survey	12.6
thermometer	4.2	ultrasonic pulse velocity kit	9.1
hygrometer	6.3	Plastics	
anemometer	7.0	Durometer	4.9
carbon dioxide detector	14.0	Brick/stone	
radon detector	15.4	ultrasonic pulse velocity kit	6.3
light meter	7.0	Flat roofs	
noise meter	15.4	leak detector	19.6

Source: Coday and Hoxley (2001).

SUMMARY

- The condition surveyor's core knowledge is a thorough understanding of construction technology.
- The surveyor needs to have this knowledge not only for modern buildings, but also for the period during which the building inspected was constructed.
- There is also a geographical dimension – the surveyor needs to know how buildings in the locality in which they survey were built over the decades and centuries.
- Patterns of failure and of typical remedial works are also essential knowledge areas.
- Specialists will need to be brought in when the surveyor strays beyond this knowledge base. Structural and building services engineers are likely to be those consulted.
- Sometimes it will be necessary to engage contractors to provide access, to open up the structure or to test drains. All of these activities will require the consent of the building owner.
- Specialist drain testing companies can be called on to provide, for example, a CCTV survey of an installation.
- Damp and timber treatment companies may sometimes be engaged, but it should always be remembered that such firms have a vested interest in recommending remedial work.
- If possible it is always better for specialists to be appointed directly by the client, but you will need to offer advice about such appointments.

Section 5
The tools of the surveyor

In this Section:

- *Equipment for surveys*
- *Investigating practice*

Introduction

Without doubt the aids that are relied on most when carrying out any form of building inspection are the surveyor's eyesight and their knowledge and experience. However, there will always be some physical equipment that the surveyor can use to assist them in both recording information and in diagnosing defects. As one would expect, there is a minimum level of equipment that must always be used when undertaking residential and commercial surveys, which is specified in the various published guidance notes (RICS, 2004a, 2005a, 2005b). These guidance notes are very explicit about what equipment must be used, and are the source to which a court of law would refer should there be any suspicion of negligence.

Equipment for surveys

The standard terms of engagement for the RICS intermediate level survey merely states: 'Equipment such as a damp-meter, binoculars and torch may be used. A ladder is used for hatches and for flat roofs not more than three metres above ground level.' However, in the guidance note to this service the RICS suggests that the list of equipment is not comprehensive and that, at their discretion, surveyors may – but are not obliged to – use other equipment (e.g. compass, tape, inspection-cover lifter, meter-box key, spirit level), and that: 'The use of cameras, while encouraged, is discretionary. There is no objection to the use of machines for recording site notes, provided that a permanent record of those notes is kept.'

Considerably more detail is provided in the RICS guidance on surveys of residential buildings and surveys of commercial and industrial buildings. This is summarised in Table 5.1.

The use to which this equipment is put is discussed in greater detail in Sections 7, 8 and 9, which are concerned with the actual inspection. Most surveyors prefer to describe the elevations of buildings by reference to their orientation, therefore a

TABLE 5.1: *A comparison of the equipment required for building surveys of residential buildings and commercial and industrial buildings*

Item of equipment	Residential building survey (RICS, 2004a)	Commercial or industrial building survey (RICS, 2005a)
Safety equipment	Hard hat Mask for inspection of loft spaces and inspection chambers First aid kit Protective overalls and gloves	Overalls, hard hat and other suitable protective clothing and footware *Disposable class FFP2 facemasks* *Goggles or light eye protection* *Gloves (latex and heavy duty)* *Ear defenders/plugs* *Cleaning materials (e.g. wet wipes) if washing facilities not available* *High-visibility vests, warning signs, protective barriers in trafficked areas*
Access	3 m ladder Lifting equipment for standard inspection chamber covers Meter-cupboard key Claw hammer and bolster	*Mobile access platforms or similar plant (usually hired in)* *Rope access services* Manhole keys *Use of contractor to open up or force access* Hammer, bolster, jemmy, crowbar
Measurement	Small tape measure or measuring rod Crack gauge or ruler Means of determining inclination of roof pitch Long tape measure Adjustable set square	2 m or 3 m tape 2 m rod 20 m or 30 m tape *In certain circumstances the use of traditional tapes can be supplemented or substituted by electronic digital measurement tools*

TABLE 5.1: *Continued*

Item of equipment	Residential building survey (RICS, 2004a)	Commercial or industrial building survey (RICS, 2005a)
Level	Spirit level Plumb bob Marble	Spirit level Plumb bob *Levels* *Theodolites*
Moisture meter	Electronic moisture meter *Moisture meter accessories, such as a surface temperature probe, a humidity sensor, an air temperature sensor* Deep insulated probes	Moisture meter
Torches	Torches Spare batteries and bulbs	Torch
Camera	Camera with flash	Camera/spare film/batteries
Binoculars	Binoculars or telescope	Binoculars, spotter scope
Recording findings	Paper, pens or pencils	Note pad/checklist (general checklist or specific to the project) Hand-held dictating or recording machine *Hand-held computer*
Compass	Compass	
Screwdriver etc.	Screwdriver, bradawl or hand-held probe Additional screwdrivers	Selection of screwdrivers, pliers
Mirror	Mirror	
Identification	Means of personal identification	
Mobile phone		Mobile phone (in case of emergencies)
Other	*Hand-held metal detector* *Borescope* *Magnifying glass*	*Cover meter* *Borescope* Chalk *Sampling bags* *Video recorder* *Gas or carbon dioxide detector*

Note: Items in *italics* are 'specialist' or optional items.

compass can be essential if surveying in an unfamiliar area on a cloudy day. A plumb line is essential for checking the verticality of walls, and a spirit level is obviously used for checking whether floors, etc. are horizontal.

Other items of equipment that the author has found useful on site include:

- a spade, for digging shallow trial holes
- protective clothing, to enable an inspection to be carried out whatever the conditions – overalls and wellington boots will usually suffice
- a camera
- drain testing equipment
- a pocket lens
- a gauge for recording crack widths
- an electric lead lamp, to be used in preference to a torch where mains electricity is available.

Each surveyor will have their own individual preferences regarding the equipment to be taken to site, but what is important is that the minimum level of equipment required to fulfil the particular conditions of engagement and as recommended by the appropriate guidance note is always carried. It is no excuse to report to a client that a roof space has not been inspected because no ladders were available.

It can sometimes be useful to carry protective clothing when inspecting the interior of a property too. Overalls and wellington boots are useful in repelling house fleas, which will continue to live in the carpets of vacant properties for some time after the other occupants have left.

Investigating practice

A few years ago, the author was involved with a funded research project to ascertain what equipment surveyors were actually using to survey the various types of building (Coday and Hoxley, 2001). The research was carried out using a postal questionnaire, which was sent, together with a stamped addressed envelope and an individually addressed covering letter, to 500 building surveyors located throughout the UK. Just under 30 per cent of the questionnaires were returned.

The main results for surveyors undertaking inspections of commercial buildings were:

- 23 per cent said that they generally or occasionally used a borescope
- 63 per cent made use of a digital camera
- 77 per cent used a speech recorder
- 48 per cent used an electronic measure
- 22 per cent used a thermometer
- 18 per cent used a hygrometer
- 19 per cent used some form of metal detector
- 24 per cent used an item of electrical testing equipment.

The main results of this study suggest that, by and large, surveyors prefer to rely on what they have relied on for centuries – their senses, and in particular their eyesight.

SUMMARY

- There is definitive guidance available on the equipment that professionals are expected to have with them when carrying out building surveys of both residential and commercial properties.
- The types of equipment summarised in Table 5.1 include that for gaining access, recording physical measurements, assessing level, checking for dampness, illuminating dark spaces (such as roof voids), and recording data collected, in addition to a camera, binoculars, a compass and a mirror.
- Failure to carry such equipment is not sufficient excuse for not inspecting.
- Other items that are sometimes useful include a spade, protective clothing, boots, drain testing equipment, pocket lens and a crack measuring gauge.
- Research suggests that increasing use is being made of items such as a borescope, metal detector and electrical testing equipment.

Section 6
How to inspect

In this Section:

- *Arriving on site*
- *Sequence of inspection*
- *Inspecting the exterior*
- *Inspecting the interior*
- *What should be recorded?*
- *How should the information be recorded?*

Arriving on site

So, the surveyor has taken instructions in writing, has organised specialists to provide assistance, has carried out preliminary research and has arrived on site with the appropriate equipment. They are now ready to undertake what is undoubtedly the most demanding of the activities involved with a survey – the actual inspection. During the early stages of an inspection it is essential for the surveyor to clear their mind so that the task in hand can be carried out with the full level of skill demanded by the client. It is likely that the surveyor will have arrived on site thinking about their previous job and so needs to forget about that and focus instead on the property to be inspected. There is no doubt that this is easier with an empty property than with one that is occupied. Where the existing owner or occupier is present during the inspection there is always the danger that the surveyor could be distracted by their presence. It is important for the surveyor to be single-minded in carrying out the inspection and to avoid anything that could lead them to lose their concentration. The other essential element of the preliminary part of a survey is for the surveyor to quickly become familiar with the property – with the extent of the building and the site.

"the '3 Fs' – focus, familiarity and freedom"

A good method of achieving all of these objectives (the '3 Fs' – focus, familiarity and freedom) is to carry out a measured survey of the plot and the building's footprint, and then to plot a sketch roof plan. This is all essential information that needs to be recorded during the inspection. By the time this fairly mechanistic and straightforward task has been completed the occupier will usually have lost interest and returned to the interior of the building, and the surveyor will be aware of the extent of the site and building and will hopefully be concentrating fully on the survey.

Sequence of inspection

Practising surveyors differ on the question of whether it is better to commence the full inspection internally or externally. Many suggest that it is better to inspect internally initially as this will cause the least inconvenience to the occupier, while others suggest that commencing with an external inspection follows more logically the order in which it is usual to report. The author favours the latter approach because if anything is missed during the initial inspection of the exterior it is an easy task to reinspect part of the exterior. It may not be as easy to reinspect the interior if any problem is suggested by the external inspection.

For example, the inspection of the roof space might reveal rain penetration around a chimney stack. If no defect had been identified during the initial external inspection of the stack, it would be an easy matter to reinspect the chimney stack flashings. However, if the roof space had been inspected first and no defect had been noticed, but the problem with the flashing was subsequently identified by the external inspection, it might be more difficult to gain access to the roof space for a second inspection (perhaps involving unscrewing a trap door, placing dust sheets and erecting a ladder).

In many respects, the order of inspection is a matter of personal preference by the surveyor. What is most important is that the inspection is carried out in a logical sequence, and that the surveyor is familiar with that sequence and is not afraid to retrace their footsteps in order to follow a trail of evidence.

"the order of inspection is a matter of personal preference"

To summarise the discussion above, the author's preferred sequence for the inspection of a property is as follows:

1 Measured survey of the plot and footprint of the building.
2 Inspection of the exterior.
3 Inspection of the interior.

Inspecting the exterior

It is best to inspect each element of construction in turn as this mirrors how the report will be structured. However, this is not always practical, particularly where the property being inspected is in the centre of a terrace. In such a situation it is necessary to inspect each elevation in turn, and indeed this is the method of recording information followed by many surveyors, even when inspecting detached or semi-detached structures. Again, such choices are largely a matter of personal preference, but whichever method is adopted it is usually best to follow the principle of starting at the top and working down. Thus, the following sequence of inspection is recommended:

1 Chimney stacks – flashings, cement fillets.
2 Roofs, pitched and flat – main slopes, abutments, ridges, hips, verges, ventilation.
3 Rainwater goods – gutters, downpipes, gulley or shoe.
4 External walls – pointing, movement joints, damp-proof course, sub-floor ventilation.
5 External joinery – fascias, soffits, windows, doors.
6 Drainage – foul, above ground, below ground, surface water.
7 Site boundaries.

What to actually record during the inspection is discussed further below and considered in greater detail in the following three sections. If the building being surveyed is large it is likely that the inspection of the exterior will take at least one or two hours. Once this is complete it is time to retreat to the interior.

Inspecting the interior

The dangers of believing any information volunteered by the vendor have been highlighted in Section 3, but there will no doubt be some matters that the surveyor wishes to clarify with the vendor. The surveyor can take this opportunity to accept a warm drink if the inspection

See: Other parties, page 25

is being carried out in cold weather (of course, an unoccupied and unheated building can be colder inside than outside, and in such situations the surveyor would be well advised to have come prepared with a flask of hot drink).

However, once the essential information has been requested of the occupier, it is time for the surveyor to regain their freedom to inspect. A useful ploy to achieve this is to commence the interior inspection in the roof space. There are other good reasons for starting in the roof space. The first is that it continues the logical sequence of starting at the top and working down. Another is that it is possible to discover more about the quality of construction in the roof space, where the builder would have made no attempt to disguise any shortcomings, than anywhere else in a building. It is also very often possible to date a building most precisely from within the roof space. While builders did not always erect a plaque on the elevation to date the building, the tradesmen often left dating evidence in the form of an engraving in a roof timber or in cement rendering to a chimney breast (or even, on some rare occasions, a discarded newspaper read during their lunch break). Finally, a relatively high number of defects or matters requiring improvement are identified in the roof space. This is an area into which many owners or occupiers never venture and they are very often not aware of the defects revealed by a survey.

The essential matters that need to be investigated during a roof space inspection are:

• structural integrity of the frame
• evidence of fungal decay or insect infestation to timber members
• condition of the undersides of roof coverings, or, where felted or boarded, the felt or boarding
• condition of gable and party walls, where applicable
• condition of chimney breasts and flues, including support provided where removed at lower levels
• type and condition of ceilings
• presence of, extent of and condition of insulation
• condition of water tanks and plumbing
• type, age and condition of electrical wiring
• evidence of rodent, bird, bat and wasp infestation
• adequate ventilation.

Once the roof-space has been inspected, each room (including circulation areas such as landings and staircases) should be inspected in detail. Again, a logical inspection sequence is recommended, such as the following:

1 Ceiling
2 Each wall (usually four)
3 Window(s)
4 Door(s)
5 Radiator, heater or fireplace
6 Electrical fittings
7 Floor

The philosophy of working downwards from the top is again followed in each room, and it is likely that the upper floors would be inspected before the ground floor (and basement if there is one), as the surveyor will already be located at upper floor level after inspecting the roof space.

What should be recorded?

The surveyor will need to be able to convert the notes made during the inspection into the report for the client. It is therefore important that the notes taken reflect what will be required in the report. For each element of construction it is necessary to record the following:

1 Design and construction
2 Condition
3 Cause of any defects (or recommend further investigation)
4 Remedial work required

An example of notes recorded during the inspection of elements of a semi-detached house are given in Figure 6.1.

Obviously, each surveyor will develop their own style of note-taking and may well abbreviate frequently used terms (if handwriting notes), but provided that each of the four points are considered in the same order for each element inspected, error-free report writing should follow.

See also:
Reporting
defects, page
111

How should the information be recorded?

There are various methods of recording information on site and each surveyor will develop their own preference. Each method is considered below:

FIGURE 6.1: *Example survey notes*

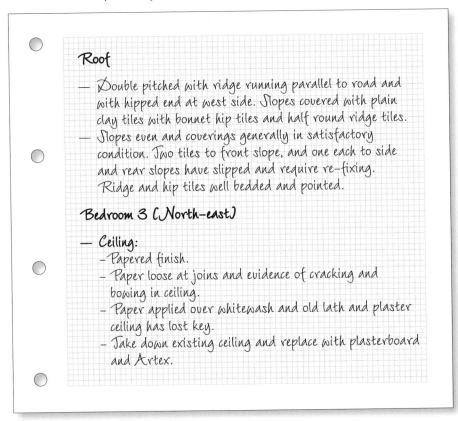

- *Taking notes by longhand* – this is obviously the most time-consuming method, but there should be a clear record of the inspection to rely on at a later date, should that be necessary.
- *Dictating notes* – using a speech recorder or MP3 player for transcription back in the office. Provided there are no recording problems, this is less time-consuming on site (most people can talk seven times faster than they can write). However, there is the delay while the notes are typed up before the report can be commenced. There is also the disadvantage of having to dictate out of hearing of the owner or occupier.
- *Making sketches* – both of the above methods can be supplemented by the use of site-prepared sketches, and many surveyors prefer to make their notes of

each elevation on a sketch of that elevation. This approach has been strongly advocated by one leading authority (Hollis, 1995b).

- *Using standard forms* – notes can be written on a preprinted form or checklist. This method saves time in that the surveyor does not need to write out most of the headings, but it can be rather cumbersome. However, the checklist approach is probably the best method for inexperienced surveyors. The checklist needs to reflect the information that will be required for the final report – an example of such a list is presented in Section 10.

  See also: Typical headings, page 114

- *Dictating the report directly on site* – either for word-processing by a secretary or directly into speech-recognition software. The latter approach is no doubt the quickest and has been adopted by many experienced surveyors, who do not like to return to the office until after their report is substantially dictated. However, in the case of *Watts v. Morrow* 1991, 4 All ER 937, CA, the judge considered that this method does not provide the surveyor the opportunity for reflective thought, which is most important when considering a property as a whole. The absence of any site notes leaves the surveyor open to a claim of negligence when adopting this method. The author suspects that those adopting this approach feel that commercial pressures outweigh the risks of being sued for negligence. No doubt a judge would look more favourably on a surveyor adopting this approach if there were some sketches with at least a minimum of annotation to record the inspection.

- *Entering data directly into a hand-held computer* – this method is only suitable for stock condition surveys, and not when any large volumes of text need to be included.

┌─────────────────────────────┐
│   **SUMMARY**   │
└─────────────────────────────┘

- When starting to inspect, some method of initial familiarisation with the building and site needs to be adopted to enable the surveyor to focus completely on the job in hand.
- The order of inspection is a matter of personal preference, but it is important to ensure that the inspection is complete and thorough. For this reason, most surveyors have a set routine that they follow.
- One such routine is for the surveyor to make an initial measured survey of the layout of the building and site, and then to inspect the exterior, followed by the interior, while in general adopting a top-down approach.
- Checklists are useful, particularly for inexperienced surveyors, to ensure that the inspection is complete and thorough.
- The roof space is a useful place to commence the inspection of the interior as it is generally a very good indication of the quality of construction.
- Note-taking for each element should record: design and construction, condition, cause of defects and then finally any remedial work required.
- Whichever method of note-taking is used, the most important principle to observe is that there should be a comprehensive record of the inspection which can be referred to, if necessary, at a later date.

Section 7
What to inspect – the essentials

In this Section:

- *Dampness*
- *Building movement*
- *Timber defects*
- *Roof coverings and structures*

Key defects

This section considers dampness, building movement, timber defects and roof coverings and structures. These defects have the greatest potential for causing the owner of a house considerable expense. Analysis of negligence claims against surveyors reveals that the claims most frequently settled by professional indemnity insurers involve these defects.

Dampness

The surveyor is required to use an electronic moisture meter to identify any dampness problems within the property. Readings should be taken at the base of ground floor internal and external walls every 1 m or so, and in any other areas throughout the property (including the roof space) where dampness is, or could be, a problem. As discussed in Section 5, it has long been a requirement that a surveyor uses a moisture meter when assessing the condition of a building. When checking for dampness in wall finishes, it is essential that the surveyor recognises that the meter actually measures electrical resistance, and that if there is any material within the wall finish that will conduct electricity (e.g. aluminium foil) then a high reading will be obtained. Should high readings be obtained in unexpected situations, where there are no visible signs of dampness, then the wall finish will need to be investigated (of course with the owner's consent).

There has been much controversy about the diagnosis of rising dampness and the use of chemically injected damp-proof courses (DPC) in recent years. It is likely that many such DPCs have been installed unnecessarily over the past 30 years or so. Many have been installed in situations where the problem was actually condensation or where an existing DPC was sound but was bridged by soil, pavings or external rendering (or perhaps imitation stone cladding) to the wall.

"some authorities question even the existence of rising dampness"

Other problems that can be confused with rising dampness are plumbing leaks and leaking rainwater goods. There are some authorities who question even the existence of the phenomenon of rising dampness. Such authorities have stood bricks in tanks of water and have been unable to notice any appreciable rise of water up the bricks. The author does not subscribe to the view that there is no such thing as rising dampness and has witnessed it in a terrace of houses built on a plinth of Staffordshire blue engineering bricks. What was happening, of course, was that dampness was not rising through the very dense and almost impermeable bricks, but through the old lime mortar. The chemical injection of a DPC into such a dense material (flint is another material where similar problems occur) is thoroughly inappropriate. In such situations, the physical insertion of a DPC may be the only option. Where the walling material is more permeable, chemical injection may be appropriate, provided that a reputable company can be engaged to carry out such work. Members of the British Wood Preserving and Damp-Proofing Association (BWPDA), which offers an insurance-backed guarantee in the event of failure, are generally reputable contractors.

When a DPC has been installed it is also necessary to replace the plaster or other finish that has been affected by dampness (the affected area is rarely more than 1 m high). The damp plaster will contain hygroscopic salts, which may continue to attract dampness from the atmosphere even after the original source of dampness is removed. When replastering, it is essential to use a cement and sand render coat, preferably with a salt inhibitor or waterproofing agent included. This can then be finished with a skim coat of a gypsum-based plaster. Sometimes, rising dampness following the installation of a DPC is due to the inappropriate use of a gypsum-based undercoat (such as Carlite) instead of a cement and sand render coat. Another common problem is that the render coat is carried down so that it is in contact with the floor – the rendering should be stopped short of the floor by about 25 mm. Some authorities (e.g. Parrett, 2006) believe that it is the cement-based render that actually damp-proofs, and that it is impossible for the injected chemicals to impregnate the bricks fully. The existence of a previously installed chemical DPC is usually evidenced by a row of small diameter holes in a brick course or courses at low level.

Most penetrating dampness problems are caused by leaking or overflowing rainwater goods, but other causes may be missing vertical DPCs or driving rain passing through poorly pointed solid walls in severely exposed locations (such as on a cliff top). Cavity fill that occupies the entire cavity can lead to penetrating dampness in similarly exposed locations. The advice to be given when dealing with a penetrating dampness problem is first to remove (or provide a barrier to) the source of dampness, and second to treat damp-affected plaster in the same way as for rising dampness.

As indicated above, condensation is often confused with rising (and indeed pene-trating) dampness, but the diagnosis of condensation is far from straightforward. Even if condensation is suspected, it is difficult to be precise about the necessary remedial work following a single inspection. This is because choices made by occupants of the property can influence the severity of the problem. Perhaps the most common problem is failure to adequately heat the dwelling – the critical average temperature

"diagnosis of condensation is far from straightforward"

is 15°C, any lower and condensation can develop. Many occupants on a low budget make the situation worse by their choice of space heating. Portable bottled gas heating appliances create large volumes of water vapour, which can increase the risk of condensation. Failure to ventilate adequately, so that moist air is removed from the building, is another contributing factor. There should be one overall air-change per hour throughout the dwelling, but high-risk areas such as bathrooms and kitchens require additional mechanical ventila-tion. Tumble driers should have ducted ventilation direct to the exterior, and cooking hob extractors should ideally have similar arrangements. One of the worst examples of roof space condensation the author has seen was caused by the occupier venting a cooker hob extractor through the ceiling of the bungalow directly into the roof space!

Since surface condensation occurs when warm air comes into contact with a cold surface (which is below the 'dew-point' temperature), another method of remedying the problem is to upgrade the thermal insulation of the wall or ceiling on which condensation is occurring. Mould growth is usually the first indication of condensation. It is essentially moisture dependent, as the other two ingredients necessary for growth (a source of infection and a source of nourishment) are always present in buildings. There are many varieties of mould, and some spores can germinate at relative humidities as low as 80 per cent. The mould will spread if the relative humidity is over 70 per cent for long periods – usually more than a 12-hour period. Remedial work will include washing the mould-affected area with a fungicidal wash or with a bleach solution, but this will only be effective in conjunction with a mixture of heating, ventilation and insulation.

Building movement

It is necessary for the surveyor to carry out careful visual inspection for signs of past or continuing building movement. This will include examining not only the building internally and externally, but also external works such as pavings, and particularly noting the location of trees and positions of drains. Where movement is detected, the extent of the problem should be noted in a level of detail sufficient to make a judgement and offer advice to the client.

Trees and drains are the two main culprits as far as subsidence is concerned – vegetation growth on shrinkable clay soils and leaking drains on mainly (but not exclusively) non-cohesive soils such as sands and gravels. As this suggests, one cannot begin to assess the causes of subsidence without knowledge of the subsoil on which the property is built, and so the surveyor should have an intimate knowledge of the geology in the area in which they practise, or should have access to detailed geological maps if surveys are carried out over a wide geographical area.

Some definitions would be useful at this point:

- *Settlement* is the natural compaction of the soil due to the load imposed by the building. It occurs soon after construction and only causes damage if it is dif-ferential – due perhaps to variations in ground conditions, old foundations or different foundation depths.
- *Subsidence* is 'the downwards movement of a building foundation caused by loss of support of the site beneath the foundations' (IStructE, 2000).

- *Heave* is the upwards movement of the soil due to its recovering its water content. This is usually caused by the removal of trees on clay soils, but can also be caused by frost action on sand or gravel soils.

Subsidence, heave and settlement (and also land-slip) are all caused by movement of the soil on which the building is founded, but building movement can also be caused by a failure of the materials of which the property is constructed. Examples of this type of failure are thermal movement, moisture movement, sulphate attack, cavity wall tie corrosion and lack of lateral restraint. Generally, movement caused by foundation failure tends to be the most serious and most expensive to remedy, so this type of movement will be considered first. Before that, however, the actual detection and assessment of movement will be considered.

Detection and assessment of building movement

Before the Second World War, most brickwork mortars contained little cement and were generally of lime and sand. Brickwork built with lime and sand mortar is able to accommodate minor movement without cracking, but the rigid-jointed brickwork of post-war property will usually crack if there is any movement. Interestingly, the author inspected a house that suffered from subsidence during the East Coast floods of the 1950s but which did not exhibit any cracking in the brickwork. The house had been constructed on a raft foundation and the raft had tilted – the entire property had a significant lean, but there was not a single crack to be seen in any external or internal wall. Such cases are unusual, however, and most post-war buildings that have suffered from foundation failure or any other type of movement will exhibit cracking.

To fully understand the current situation regarding the weight given to cracking when assessing movement of residential buildings it is necessary to view the problem from an insurance industry perspective. Settlement is not and never has been covered by domestic insurance policies; subsidence has been covered by most policies since about 1971, while heave is covered by some policies.

Following the long hot summers of 1976, 1989 and 1995 there were significant increases in the numbers of claims made on insurance policies. A large proportion of the cost of these claims, particularly following the 1976 damage, was for foundation underpinning which many experts believe was unnecessary. To provide an objective framework for assessing damage, Building Research Establishment (BRE) Digest 251 was introduced in 1981 (and amended in

1995). The digest, entitled *Assessment of Damage in Low-rise Buildings,* presents six categories of damage, ranging from 0 (negligible) to 5 (the most severe, where cracks are over 25mm in width). See Table 7.1. BRE Digest 251 emphasises that crack width is just one factor in assessing the category of damage, but the information in Table 7.1 is useful as it gives an indication of the likely repair works for the six categories of damage.

Despite the objective information provided by BRE Digest 251, some unnecessary underpinning still goes on today. This is partly due to pressure brought by policy-holders who are unwilling to accept the BRE's advice that cracks up to say 5 mm in width are nothing to worry about, but also due to the wish for a quick fix – a once and for all repair that does away with the need for prolonged monitoring of the movement. Research by one experienced insurance loss adjuster, who looked at 282 cases of subsidence damage, revealed that the only factor that was consistently of relevance to the decision to underpin was the actual size of the crack (Wilkin and Baggott, 1994).

"unnecessary underpinning still goes on today"

When assessing building movement the surveyor must initially categorise the damage in accordance with BRE Digest 251. The precise locations and sizes of cracks should be noted, and in most instances it will be necessary to sketch the affected elevations and any damaged walls and ceilings internally. It takes considerable experience to be able to identify the width of a crack without physically measuring it. The best way to measure cracks is with a crack width gauge. Sketching serves two purposes. First, it provides a record of the damage at the time of inspection so that if the surveyor is called back many months later it will be possible to determine whether any further movement has occurred. Second, by preparing sketches, such as that shown in Figure 7.1, the surveyor will begin to develop an awareness of how the building is moving. Cracking due to foundation movement usually extends above and below the DPC, affects both internal and external surfaces, is usually diagonal in direction and is usually tapered (i.e. of uneven width). It is in the assessment of tapered cracks that the surveyor should be able to see whether various parts of the building are moving up or down in relation to one another (see Figure 7.2). Obviously, the correct diagnosis of the direction of movement is essential as it is necessary to differentiate between subsidence and heave and to determine which parts of the building are affected by the movement.

TABLE 7.1: *Classification of visible damage to walls with particular reference to ease of repair of plaster and brickwork or masonry*
(Crack width is just one factor in assessing category of damage and should not be used on its own as a direct measure of it)

Damage category	Description of typical damage	Typical size of crack	Ease of repair
0	Hairline cracks classed as negligible	Less than about 0.1 mm	No action required
1	Fine cracks with damage generally restricted to internal wall finishes; cracks rarely visible in external brickwork	Up to 1 mm	Treated easily using normal decoration
2	Cracks not necessarily visible externally; doors and windows may stick slightly	Up to 5 mm	Cracks easily filled; recurrent cracks can be masked by suitable linings; some external pointing may be required to ensure weather-tightness; doors and windows may require easing and adjusting
3	Doors and windows sticking; service pipes may fracture; weather tightness often impaired	5 to 15 mm (or several of say 3 mm)	Cracks require some opening up and can be patched by a mason; repointing of external brickwork and possibly a small amount of brickwork to be replaced
4	Extensive damage, especially over doors and windows; windows and door frames distorted, floor sloping noticeably,* walls leaning or bulging noticeably,* some loss of bearing in beams; service pipes disrupted	15 to 25 mm (but depends on number of cracks)	Requires breaking-out and replacing sections of walls
5	Structural damage; beams lose bearing, walls lean badly and require shoring; windows broken with distortion; danger of instability	Greater than 25 mm (but depends on number of cracks)	Requires a major repair job, involving partial or complete rebuilding

* Local deviation of slope, from horizontal or vertical, of more than 1/100 will normally be clearly visible. Overall deviations in excess of 1/150 are undesirable.

Source: Copyright BRE, reproduced from BRE Digest 251 with permission.

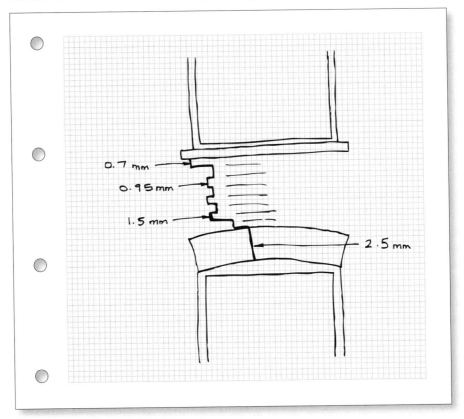

Once the cracking has been recorded and categorised it is then necessary to determine the likely age of the cracks. This is not as easy as it sounds. In areas of heavy pollution, the interior surfaces of a recent crack should be lighter in colour than the face of the wall. If there is dirt, moss or other vegetation evident inside the crack then it is likely to be older. Internally, the age of decorations can give a clue as to the age of the crack. If the decoration is old and there is evidence of previous filling of the crack then it is safe to assume that the crack is old. However, it may still be moving (see below). If the decoration is recent and the crack seems to have developed since the redecoration then it is likely to be a recent crack. If the survey is being performed for the owner then it may be possible to obtain more reliable information than when surveying for a potential purchaser. Some owners are very forthcoming and will say exactly when the crack

FIGURE 7.2: *Typical foundation movement cracking*

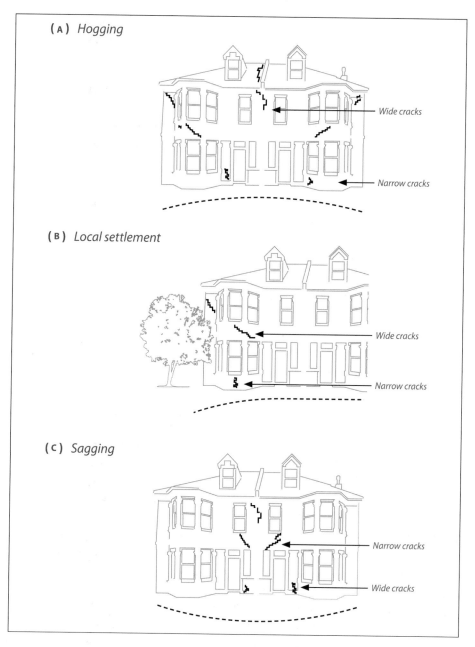

Source: based on Figure 13 in CIRIA Report 111 (1986), reproduced with permission.

appeared. The author was called out by one owner to investigate a 25-mm wide crack that had appeared overnight in the internal wall between the main front and rear rooms of the house and which seemed to be growing larger every second. In this case, it proved fairly easy to discover that the crack had been caused by a burst water main under the house, which was founded on a sand subsoil. Unfortunately, not all building movement problems are this easy to diagnose!

If the surveyor concludes that the movement has been caused by foundation movement and that it appears recent, the next question to be asked is 'what is causing the movement?'. As indicated at the beginning of this section, the two main causes are trees and drains, and these are discussed in more detail below. If either of these two hazards is present in close proximity to the area of damage then it is appropriate to recommend further investigation. Such investigation is likely to involve digging trial holes, testing the watertightness of drain runs and, if trees are suspected, possibly calling in an arboriculturist. Once the cause of the movement is removed or alleviated, it will then be necessary to monitor the building over a period of time before deciding on the necessary remedial works. Clearly, such further investigation and monitoring is beyond the scope of the original instructions if these were merely to carry out a survey. The surveyor's professional duty is to record the extent of the movement at the time of the survey, to say whether they think it is recent, to suggest possible causes and to recommend appropriate further investigations.

Other causes of foundation failure are landslip – where one expanse of soil moves in relation to another (usually downhill) – and mining subsidence. A surveyor practising in an area where mining has taken place in the past will no doubt be aware of the locations of most workings and will have access to a map showing the principal mines. Not all workings are indicated on these maps, however, and some small shafts worked for only short periods by small companies may not be properly recorded. The two principal causes of foundation failure – leaking drains and trees – will now be considered in more detail.

Drains

Most drains laid before 1970 had rigid socket and spigot joints formed with cement – such drains are not able to accommodate ground movement. Plastic-sleeved joints were used on rigid pipes from about 1970, and flexible uPVC drains with flexible joints have been used for the past 15–20 years. There was a short period during the 1960s when pitch fibre pipes were commonly installed, and many of these pipes have suffered from either blockage or leakage due to being compressed by the weight of soil. The author practised for many years on the coast in Norfolk, where a combination of rigid-jointed drains and non-cohesive soils (originally beach sand) led to many subsidence problems in pre-1960 properties.

Where there are trees and shrubs close to drain runs, roots can further damage a slightly leaking drain and so the presence of roots should be checked for in inspection chambers. If there are drains close to the area of damage then the watertightness of the drains should be checked. If the drains are leaking then it will be necessary to repair, or more likely replace, these. The cracking should then be monitored, and if no further movement occurs then the cracks can be repaired and any other necessary remedial works carried out. Only when there has been severe leakage that has washed away the soil beneath foundations will further movement occur, necessitating the underpinning of foundations. It is important to note that most buildings insurance policies do not cover damaged pipes and so drain repairs do not form a legitimate expense under any claim. What is covered by most policies is damage caused by leaking pipes, and therefore the cost of any underpinning and the cosmetic repair work can be recovered. Perhaps this is another reason why much under-pinning has been carried out unnecessarily in the past! It should also be noted that building control approval is required for drain replacement work.

"most buildings insurance policies do not cover damaged pipes"

Trees

The predominant subsoil type in the south-east of England is shrinkable clay, but it was not until after the 1976 drought that the Building Regulations were amended to require a minimum foundation depth of 1.0 m on clay soils. Where there are trees or vegetation close to a proposed building on a clay subsoil then the foundation depth is required to be very much deeper, so that they extend below any root growth – this usually involves the use of trench fill or piled foundations. It is generally accepted that global warming will increase the frequency of extreme weather events. It is therefore possible that more severe droughts than we have experienced to date will lead to subsidence problems in many pre-1980 houses that have so far shown no sign of any problem. Similarly, as trees grow and extract more water from clay subsoils in drought conditions it is likely that there will continue to be more subsidence problems due to desiccation of the soil.

Trees are an important part of the urban landscape and if all trees that could adversely affect buildings were to be removed then this landscape would be destroyed in many of our towns and cities. The traditional advice about the proximity of trees to buildings on clay subsoils is that the tree should be at least its mature height from any buildings, and where there are groups of trees then these should be at least one and a half times their mature height away. Of course, not all trees present the same risk. The species that extract the most water from the soil include poplar, willow, oak, elm, horse chestnut and sycamore. This fact requires the surveyor to be able to identify trees. The author has sometimes found this difficult using traditional books and prefers to use the swatch book of tree leaves reproduced to their actual sizes that the Woodland Trust sells for about £5 (Woodland Trust, 2008). Parnham and Rispin (2001) cite research that suggests the traditional guidance on the distances from tree to building may be overcautious. They report that an insurance company has discovered that 90 per cent of damage to property on shrinkable soils occurred when the trees were within the following distances:

- 20 m for high water demand trees
- 10 m for medium water demand trees.

Of course, if a mature tree were discovered to be causing subsidence it is not possible merely to remove it, as the resultant increase in water content of the soil would cause heave to occur. A possible solution would be for the height of the tree to be reduced gradually. The surveyor would probably feel obliged to recommend that the client consult an arboriculturist if such a solution is proposed.

Trees can cause other problems apart from subsidence on clay soils. Their leaves can block gutters, including vulnerable internal valley and parapet gutters, and buildings can be badly damaged by falling trees.

Secondary causes of movement

As mentioned above, less serious but equally substantial movement can occur as a result of problems with the method of construction. Generally, cracking from such defects does not extend below the DPC, and the pattern of the cracking enables these defects to be identified. The main causes are as follows:

- *Thermal movement of masonry walls* – Large expanses of traditional clay brickwork require vertical movement joints to allow for thermal expansion and contraction. Joints should be provided at 12 m centres. Defects due to inadequate provision of expansion joints are particularly prevalent in terraces, where vertical cracks will be seen at the weakest points – generally above and below window openings. Remedial works are difficult because movement will continue unless a physical expansion joint is installed. The extent of cracking is usually small and does not warrant the expense of forming such a joint.
- *Moisture movement of masonry* – The most common example of this type of movement is the drying shrinkage of calcium silicate (sand-lime) bricks. Unless movement joints are provided when using such bricks, some cracking will usually occur. The cracking generally follows the mortar joints with no sign of vertical displacement, and these joints can be repointed once the cracking has occurred. Since sand-lime bricks have smooth faces and are of a very regular and consistent size and shape, the repointed joints always look rather unsightly.
- *Sulphate attack of clay brickwork* – Naturally occurring sulphates in the clay from which the bricks are formed combine with a by-product of the cement in the mortar to produce calcium sulpho-aluminate. The crystals of this material expand when wet, causing expansion of the brickwork. This results in cracking in joints, and sometimes bulging, both of which are more pronounced towards the top of the wall, which is generally wetter. Sulphate attack is mainly a problem in chimney stacks and parapet walls, but it can also affect external walls of buildings. If the problem persists then repointing with a sulphate-resisting cement may be necessary. Efflorescence is a much less serious problem – the white deposits, caused by salts being brought to the surface of new clay brickwork by rain, will eventually disappear or can be brushed off.
- *Cavity wall tie corrosion* – Research by the BRE suggests that any cavity wall built before the standard for the galvanising of steel ties was upgraded in 1981 is likely to fail before the expected life of the building is reached. Cavity walls were adopted generally in the UK in the interwar period, but there are earlier examples dating to before the beginning of the 20th century. Early wall ties were often formed from iron or steel with no protective coating whatsoever. Later examples were protected with a coat of bitumen. Corrosion

and expansion of the ferrous metal causes horizontal cracking in the bed joints in which the ties are located. Thus there will be horizontal cracks in every sixth course or so. The cracking will be more pronounced on exposed elevations and towards the top of the wall where the weight of the wall is less. Some of the worst examples of wall tie failure are to be found on exposed coasts, where the salt-laden air causes greater corrosion. If repointing of occasional horizontal joints is evident during the inspection then wall tie corrosion should be suspected. Occasionally, the wall will bulge outwards, and in such instances some rebuilding may be required. It is more usual, however, to remove the corroded ties and to substitute stainless steel ties, often embedded in epoxy resin and then tensioned. A whole industry has developed to carry out this work, and as with any other activity a reputable contractor should be recommended. The appropriate further investigation work to recommend if wall tie failure is suspected is for a borescope inspection to be carried out by a reputable specialist contractor.

- *Lack of lateral restraint* – It is slightly more than 30 years since the Building Regulations were amended to require lateral restraint to be provided to external walls at floor and roof level. In a building built before the mid 1980s, some form of bulging may be expected in a flank wall where the joists (in particular the floor joists) run parallel to the wall. The problem is often accentuated by the presence of the stairs adjacent to this wall. The extent of bulging should be measured with the aid of a plumb line. CIRIA (1986) offers the following advice as to the stability of bulging walls:
  - Where the wall is not well restrained, it retains a precarious equilibrium with leans or bulges of up to 85 per cent of wall thickness (assuming a solid wall) provided it supports no loading from an upper storey or beam.
  - With adequate restraint, the wall will support a concentric load while still retaining a precarious equilibrium at leans or bulges of up to 85 per cent of wall thickness.
  - An unrestrained wall supporting a concentric load reaches precarious equilibrium at 50 per cent of wall thickness.

  See Figure 7.3 for an illustration of these principles. This advice provides comfort for many investigators, and inspires ideas for strengthening walls that are poorly restrained (Robson, 1999).

- *Roof spread* – This is another relatively common problem that can cause bulging and cracking of masonry walls. The spread is sometimes caused by re-roofing with a heavier covering than existed previously without strengthening the

FIGURE 7.3: *Stability of freestanding and restrained walls*

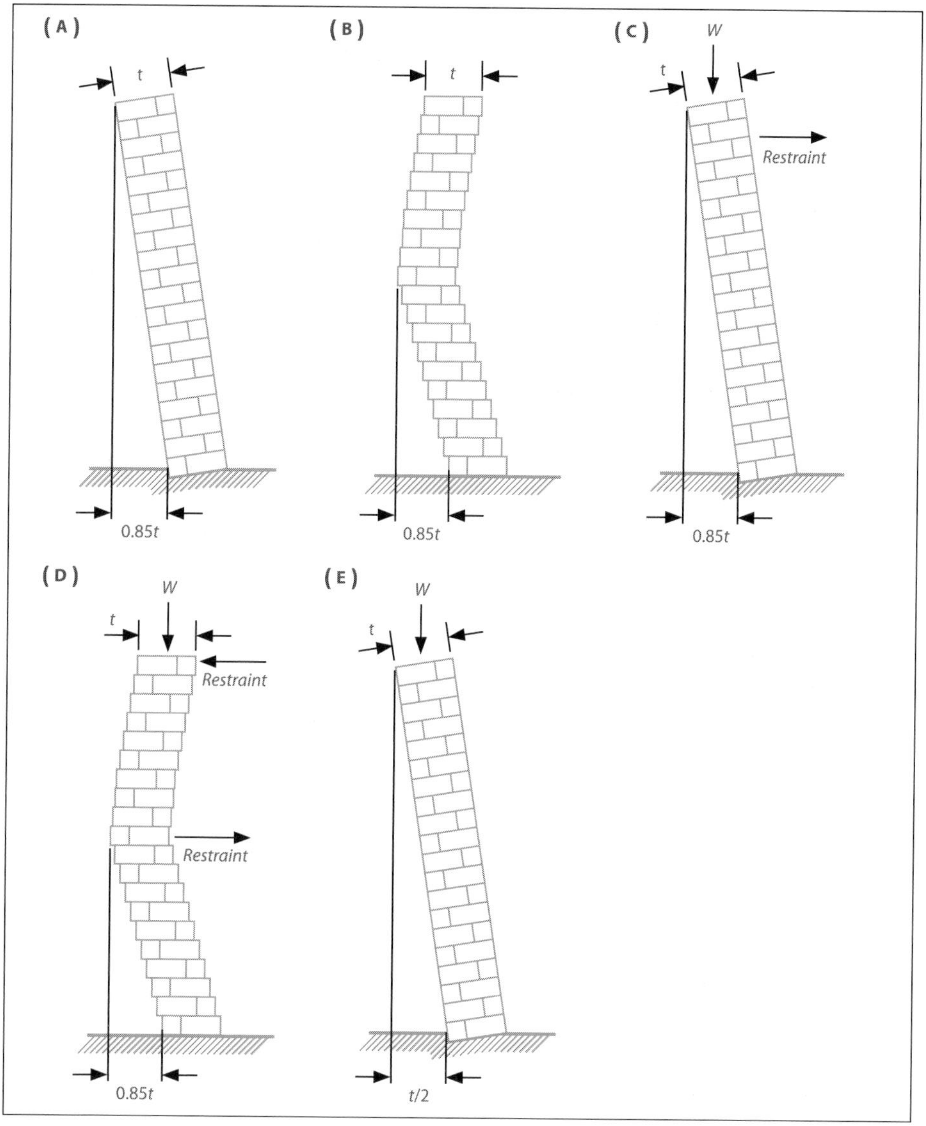

Source: based on Figure 12 in CIRIA Report 111 (1986), reproduced with permission.

roof structure and sometimes by alteration or deterioration of the roof structure. The worst example of roof spread that the author has witnessed was the result of the *tenant* of a bungalow deciding to remove some rather important trussed rafter members in order to increase the room available in the roof space for a model railway! With a similar but less serious problem it is common to see relatively minor cracking at high level to walls to which the roof is not tied down. This is caused by slight uplift of the roof during very heavy wind loading and in most instances is not serious enough to warrant remedial work.

Monitoring movement

Reference has been made earlier in this section to the need to monitor building movement over time. In addition to the careful recording of the length, width and pattern of cracks it is necessary to measure the extent of movement on either side of the cracks. This is best done by fixing studs with epoxy resin into the masonry on either side of the cracks (two on one side of each crack and one on the other side). By taking precise measurements of the sides of the triangle between the centres of the studs at regular intervals, the extent of any movement can be assessed. An alternative is to use proprietary calibrated tell-tales, but in the author's experience these are not always clear to read and are more easily affected by the weather and vandals. The least effective method is to use glass tell-tales, which will only tell you one thing if they break – that the building has moved!

Timber defects

The surveyor should carry out a careful visual inspection of a reasonable proportion of the accessible timber surfaces (internally and externally) for evidence of any past or continuing defects, such as rot or woodworm. The timber components should be tested with an electronic moisture meter calibrated to record the percentage moisture content of the timber.

Timber defects can be divided into those caused by insect infestation and those caused by fungal attack. The advice for the treatment of timber defects has changed significantly within recent years in response to concerns about the extent of damage caused by the removal of sound timber and environmental concerns about the amounts and types of chemicals that have been used in the past. These chemicals have been shown to be harmful to animals that live in and around buildings and also to the building's human occupants. Some of the most up-to-date advice on the detection and remediation of timber defects is to be found in a BRE document (Bravery *et al.*, 2003). A brief summary of the essential matters a surveyor requires to know is as follows.

Wood-boring insects

A number of insects (mainly beetles) are able to use wood as a food source and some can cause serious damage to building timbers. The typical life cycle is: larva (worm), 1–5 years; pupa (larva to adult), 6 weeks; adult (beetle), 2–3 weeks. The adult female mates and lays eggs on the surface of, or in crevices in, wood to start the cycle again. Insects can be classified into those where insecticidal treatment is usually needed and those where treatment is necessary only to control the associated wood rot. In the latter case, the insects (e.g. bees, wasps, weevils and wharf borer, tenebrionid and stag beetles) only attack rotten timber. Insects that require insecticidal treatment are considered below:

- *Common furniture beetle (*Anobium punctatum*) –* the most common type of infestation and commonly known by the name 'woodworm'. Can attack softwood and European hardwoods, but only the sapwood of sound timber. Frequently found in older furniture, in roof voids, in staircases and in floor timbers that are slightly damp. Flight holes are circular and 1–2 mm in diameter, and bore dust (frass) is cream-coloured, comprises lemon-shaped pellets and is gritty when rubbed between the fingers. Remedial treatment usually involves organic solvent, emulsion or paste.
- *Lyctus powderpost beetle (*Lyctus brunneus*) –* attacks sapwood of tropical and European hardwoods, principally oak and elm. Not found in softwoods. Common in furniture, and occasionally found in block or strip flooring. Flight holes are circular, 1–2 mm in diameter. Tunnels close to the surface are a feature of attack. Frass is cream-coloured, fine and talc-like. Remedial treatment involves organic solvent or paste.
- *House longhorn beetle* – attacks sapwood of most timbers (particularly roofing timbers). At present it is only common in Surrey, where special Building Regulations exist. It is rare in other parts of the country. The author is aware of one infestation in a Norfolk seaside town, however the beetles had been introduced into the property as a result of the occupiers moving (with their furniture) from Surrey. Flight holes large and oval, often ragged, 6–10 mm. Extensive infestations have been discovered by hearing larvae feeding. Frass comprises cream-coloured, sausage-shaped pellets. Remedial treatment involves organic solvent or paste. Structural timbers often require replacement. BRE must be notified of every attack.
- *Deathwatch beetle (*Xestobium rufovillosum*) –* attacks sapwood and heartwood of partially decayed hardwood, mainly oak. Often found in historic

buildings, and dampness is essential for establishment and for rapid development. Flight holes are circular, 2–3 mm, with extensive tunnelling. Frass comprises cream-coloured, disc-shaped pellets, and is gritty when rubbed between fingers. Remedial treatment involves organic solvent or paste (sometimes smoke). The principal remedial measure is to reduce dampness – an EU-funded study by English Heritage has suggested that preservative treatments are ineffective and that it is more important to solve the dampness problems. New timbers may be placed alongside the affected timbers.

- *Ptilinus beetle (*Ptilinus pectinicornis*)* – affects a limited range of European hardwoods – mainly beech, elm, hornbeam and maple. Mainly found in furniture. Flight holes are circular, 1–2 mm. Cream-coloured frass is very densely packed in tunnels and not easily dislodged. The frass is fine, feeling talc-like when crushed and rubbed between the fingers. Treatment may be with organic solvent, emulsion or paste.
- *Subterranean termites* – discovered in the south-west of England about ten years ago (global warming is thought to be a contributory factor). Termites rapidly eat timber-framed structures and the government quickly carried out an urgent eradication programme.

Fungal attack

Wood-rotting fungi feed off timber with a moisture content above 20 per cent and therefore only occur internally in buildings if there is a dampness problem. The most common causes of dampness are rising or penetrating dampness and leaking rainwater goods or plumbing.

Main types of wood-rotting fungi are:

- *white rots* – cause wood to become lighter in colour and fibrous in texture, without cross-cracking
- *brown rots* – cause the wood to become darker in colour, and to crack along and across the grain. When dry, very decayed wood will crumble to dust.

Except for one brown rot, *Serpula lacrymans*, which is commonly known as 'dry rot', all white rots and brown rots are referred to as 'wet rots'.

Wet rots can affect softwoods and hardwoods, are relatively rare internally, but are common on external joinery. Although there are several types of both white and brown rots, identification is sometimes difficult. However, identification is not crucial since the remedial measures are the same for all wet rots:

1 Establish the size and significance of the attack. In particular, if structural timbers are affected a detailed investigation should be carried out to ascertain whether structural repairs are necessary and, if they are, take steps to secure structural integrity.
2 Locate and eliminate sources of moisture.
3 Promote rapid drying of the structure.
4 Remove rotted wood. Apply localised preservative treatment only to timbers that are likely to remain damp for long periods.
5 In replacement work, use preservative-treated timbers.
6 Introduce support measures, for example ventilation pathways between sound timber and wet brickwork, or, where ventilation is not possible, provide a barrier such as a damp-proof membrane or joist-hangers between timber and wet brickwork.

Dry rot mostly affects softwood and often causes extensive damage. Remedial works can be very expensive. It is sensitive to high temperatures (over 25°C) and drying and is therefore rarely found on exposed timbers or in situations where fluctuating conditions are likely (such as well-ventilated sub-floor voids or roof spaces). It is able to grow through bricks and mortar but requires timber to feed on. Strands can transport moisture from damp areas, allowing the fungus to spread to dry wood in unventilated conditions. Appearance of the fruiting body may be the first indication of an outbreak. Decayed wood has a dull brown colour, typically with deep cracks along and across the grain, is light in weight and crumbles between the fingers. There is no skin of sound wood. The fungal characteristics are silky white sheets or cotton wool-like mycelium, white to grey strands (sometimes as thick as a pencil), yellow or red fruiting body with white or grey edges and profuse reddish brown dust spores.

The remedial treatment for dry rot is as follows:

1 Establish the size and significance of the attack. In particular, if structural timbers are affected a detailed investigation should be carried out to ascertain whether structural repairs are necessary – and if they are, take steps to secure structural integrity.
2 Locate and eliminate sources of moisture.
3 Promote rapid drying of the structure.
4 Remove rotted wood, cutting away timber approximately 300–450 mm from the last evidence of fungus or rot.

5 Contain the fungus within the wall using preservatives in cases where drying will be delayed.

6 In replacement work, use preservative-treated timbers.

7 Treat remaining sound timbers that are at risk with preservative (minimum two full brush coats).

8 Introduce support measures, for example ventilation pathways between sound timber and wet brickwork, or, where ventilation is not possible, providing a barrier such as a damp-proof membrane or joist-hangers between timber and wet brickwork.

9 Do not retain timber that has been infected by dry rot without seeking expert advice. There is always a risk in retaining infected wood, which can be minimised by preservative treatment and subsequent inspection (Bravery *et al.*, 2003).

As discussed in Section 4, it is one of the core skills of the surveyor to be able to detect both insect infestation and fungal attack of timber, but once detected the advice should always be that a specialist timber treatment company able to offer an insurance-backed guarantee should be engaged to carry out the remedial work. Since dry rot remedial works are usually very expensive, the advice of such a specialist should be obtained before entering into a contract to purchase a property affected by dry rot.

When assessing the condition of painted softwood external joinery, it is important to use a penknife or other probe to check for wet rot attack and the presence of filler. It is possible for the surface of, for example, a window cill to appear perfectly fine only for there to be extensive rot or filler beneath. When reporting on wet rot attack to external joinery it is often better not to be too specific about where attack has been detected. If, for instance, rot is discovered in three out of eight windows in a house, the client will no doubt express some disquiet if they discover rot in a fourth window. It would be better to report something like 'extensive wet rot is evident and has affected several windows, including those of the dining room, study and bathroom'.

Roof coverings and structures

| See also: Equipment for surveys, page 37 |

The residential survey guidance notes considered earlier require the surveyor to carry a set of ladders capable of accessing flat roofs up to 3 m above ground level. Pitched roofs above this level should be inspected from the ground through binoculars, but it may be necessary to gain access to neighbouring properties to facilitate this. A careful visual inspection of all accessible and visible roof coverings and structures, such as chimney stacks and pots, for any evidence of past or continuing defects should be undertaken. Upper roofs will be inspected from the ground through binoculars. All accessible roof voids should be inspected so that the construction and condition can be assessed.

In this context, the word 'structures' refers to any structure above roof level. In addition to chimney stacks, it could include parapet walls, roof-lights, dormer windows, structures to house observation towers and so on.

Roof coverings

It is important to inspect both the upper and under surfaces of a roof covering before advising on any repair or replacement works. The absence of sarking felt or the presence of delamination of the underside of roof slates or tiles may have a bearing on the eventual advice given to the client. It is wise to see what has happened to similar neighbouring houses. If most properties in the street have been re-roofed then it is fairly safe to assume that the building being inspected will also require re-roofing in the near future if it does not already have a new roof covering.

In addition to considering the overall condition of the main roof covering and its expected life, it is important that the edge details of the roof are inspected. Ridge, verge, hip, valley and abutment details should all be considered. Ventilation (or in older roofs the probable lack of it) should be considered and appropriate advice offered. A roof that is in otherwise satisfactory condition may require re-bedding of ridge tiles or replacement of abutment lead flashings which have been provided in overly large sections and which have therefore suffered from thermal movement.

Flat roofs

Flat roofs should be treated with great caution. The expected life of a timber-framed flat roof with an old BS 747 felt covering is, at the most, ten years. Better quality high-performance roofing felts have been used for a number of years, but even these have a maximum life of 15–20 years from new. The presence of ventilation is most important with a cold roof deck, and the lack of ventilation in a roof known to have a cold deck should lead the surveyor to report that the roof structure and deck may well be in poor condition. An assessment of the condition of the covering, the effectiveness of any solar reflective finish, the presence of ventilation and the condition of abutment details should allow the surveyor to give an indication of the likely life expectancy of the flat roof. Experience suggests that it is always better to be pessimistic in this assessment.

Chimney stacks

Chimney stack defects to check for include:

- leaning stacks, which may require rebuilding
- sulphate attack, which can often contribute to the stack leaning
- poorly pointed brickwork
- defective or missing lead flashings (cement mortar fillets may have been provided in inferior construction)
- precariously balanced pots and flaunching.

Binoculars are particularly useful for inspecting stacks. Where a gas appliance is installed then a stainless steel flue terminal is evidence that the brick flue *may* have been lined.

Roof spaces

The importance of the roof space inspection was emphasised in Section 6. The essential matters that need to be investigated during a roof space inspection are discussed in greater detail below:

- *Structural integrity of the frame* – This is undoubtedly the most important item. Timber member sizes and approximate spans should be recorded so that these can be checked back in the office. Any evidence of excessive deflection or poorly formed joints should be noted. The joints between rafter feet and ceiling joists are particularly important to ensure that no spreading of the roof is occurring. Where there are trussed rafters, the wind bracing and lateral restraint arrangements should be checked (the earliest trussed rafters had neither).
- *Evidence of fungal decay and insect infestation to timber members* – These items have been discussed above. If evidence of woodworm is discovered then signs of recent attack (fresh frass) should be investigated. It should be borne in mind,

however, that such evidence might appear even after an infestation has been treated. This is because the beetles might still emerge before being killed by the preservative treatment.

- *Condition of the underside of roof coverings or, where felted or boarded, the felt or boarding* – Tears or gaps in felt should be checked for. When inspecting during snow, do not be surprised to discover some of this in the roof space – snow can be blown through small gaps through which rain will not penetrate.
- *Condition of gable and party walls where applicable* – The author has discovered evidence of cavity wall tie corrosion on a gable wall that was not readily detectable from an external inspection from ground level.
- *Condition of chimney breasts and flues* – including support provided where removed at lower levels. It is surprising how many chimney breasts are inadequately supported in roof spaces (support off slender ceiling joists is quite common). Remedial works to be recommended will usually involve support by a steel beam. The flues should be checked to ensure that they do not communicate with the roof space. If they do then lining of the flues should be recommended.
- *Type and condition of ceilings* – Where lath and plaster (or even reed and plaster) ceilings exist, the limited life of these should be reported on.
- *Presence of, extent of and condition of insulation* – Around 250–300 mm thickness of insulation is the norm for new houses. The eaves should be checked to ensure that insulation does not block ventilation gaps.
- *Condition of water tanks and plumbing* – see Section 8.
- *Type, age and condition of electrical wiring* – see Section 8.
- *Evidence of rodent, bird, bat and wasp infestation*– see Section 9.
- *Adequate ventilation* – If the roof space is well insulated then ventilation should be recommended if it is not present.

The inspection of the roof space is sometimes hampered because there is an attic room formed within it. The surveyor should check details of the floor joists, staircase access and natural lighting to ensure that the room has been provided in accordance with Building Regulations. Where it is obvious that the loft conversion is a DIY project then this fact should be reported to the client together with the advice that the room is only suitable for light storage purposes. As far as possible, the surveyor should check to ensure that the DIY efforts have not weakened the structure of the original roof. Where only opening up works would confirm this fact then such works should be recommended.

SUMMARY

- The experience of PI insurers suggests that defects involving dampness, building movement, timber rot or infestation, roof structures and roof coverings are the most significant in terms of surveyor error.
- The surveyor is required to use an electronic moisture meter to detect rising dampness, penetrating dampness and condensation.
- Cracking in walls can be associated with ground movement or with the deterioration of the walling materials.
- The most common causes of ground movement are the effects of vegetation on clay soils or of leaking drains on sand soils.
- Secondary causes of movement are thermal effects, moisture effects, sulphate attack, cavity wall tie corrosion, lack of lateral restraint and spreading of the roof.
- Timber defects are associated with insect infestation or fungal attack. The most significant defect, in terms of damage and remediation, is dry rot. Most timber defects require a relatively high level of dampness to become established.
- The surveyor is required to carry ladders capable of reaching the eaves of single-storey structures. Above that level, roof coverings, chimney stacks, etc. should be inspected through binoculars.
- Roof space inspections are required to investigate the structural integrity of the frame, timber defects, the condition of roof coverings, gable and party walls, chimney breasts and flues, upper floor ceilings, insulation, services and evidence of rodent, bird or insect infestation.

Section 8
What to inspect – services and environment

In this Section:

- *Electrical installations*
- *Heating and associated installations*
- *Plumbing installations*
- *Underground drainage systems*
- *Above ground drainage and rainwater systems*
- *Gas installations and oil storage*
- *Other services*
- *Environmental issues*
- *Insulation*

Introduction

The surveyor is expected to carry out a visual examination, without tests, of the services that are readily accessible without risk of causing damage to the property or injury to the surveyor. The condition of the services should be assessed and any obvious non-compliance with safety or other regulations identified. The client should be advised of the need for further tests and examinations by appropriate specialists. The types of service installations inspected will normally include:

- electricity
- gas

- plumbing
- heating
- drainage.

Sufficient information should be collected to advise on:

- health and safety issues
- significant defects
- requirements for further tests.

This may require the inspection of service elements in voids and ducts, such as roof spaces, below floor voids, in basements and in tank rooms, cupboards or service ducts.

Many surveyors do not consider that the services of the building are their responsibility and carry out the most casual of inspections. This approach has been challenged, and it has been suggested that surveyors need to be far more proactive and practical in their advice about services (Parnham and Rispin, 2001, pp 229–230). This certainly mirrors the situation of US Home Inspectors, who often *test* services. For the time being, however, UK surveyors are to *inspect* but not *test* the services.

Electrical installations

The visual inspection should include:

- the identification of the type, age and general condition of the visible cabling in all accessible locations
- the location and inspection of the meters and associated switchgear
- the inspection of a sample of the switches, sockets, fittings and fixed appliances.

The inspection should allow the surveyor to prepare a general assessment of condition and suitability without any form of test.

One of the Cambridge colleges proudly proclaims in its prospectus that its dining room has never had an electricity supply connected and that students may dine by candlelight every evening during term. This building must be one of only a very few in the 21st century, but when the author started surveying buildings just over 30 years ago it was not uncommon to discover a house that was still lit by gas and which had no electricity supply connected. It is only just over 100 years since the first electricity supply was made available, and in 1914 most houses did not have a supply. It was only in the interwar period that there was a large-scale move from gas to electrical lighting – and of course electricity could also power appliances.

Electricity is one of the subjects that many surveyors have difficulty in understanding. A brief summary of the essential points is presented here.

Regulations

The IEE Wiring Regulations (BSI, 2008) are now adopted as the industry standard and are concerned with the design, installation and testing of electrical circuits. Although not statutory, they do constitute good practice, and electricity companies will only supply electricity to houses wired to the standard set out in the Regulations. In addition, Part P of the Building Regulations is also concerned with the safety of electrical installations of dwellings. The IEE Wiring Regulations cover polarity, earthing, insulation resistance and circuit continuity.

Electrical supply

In the past, some houses had overhead electrical supplies, but the vast majority now have underground supplies. The meter and the consumer unit (which contains the fuses) were traditionally placed inside the house. Today, the incoming supply cable usually terminates in a cabinet placed on the outside of the house (so that the electricity company can read the meter externally and, if necessary, disconnect the supply), while the consumer unit remains inside the house. The cabinet contains a sealed fuse designed to blow if the fuses in the consumer unit fail to operate. The consumer unit contains the mains switch, which isolates all the circuits in the house. Each circuit within the building will have its own fuse or circuit breaker.

Circuits

The power circuits of a property built before the Second World War were generally arranged using a radial system – individual cables were fed from the fuse box to one or more socket outlets. The individual circuits were wired and fused for differing purposes, such as one circuit for small electrical equipment and another for larger equipment. Modern-day installations have a ring main system, whereby the cable consisting of the live, neutral and earth wires runs from the fuse in the consumer unit, serving each socket or appliance in turn, returning in a ring to the consumer unit. There is usually one ring for each floor of the building. As the power flows both ways round the ring, the load on the cable is reduced – which permits smaller cable sizes. The total load for a ring main is usually 30 A. It is unlikely that all sockets will be used at any one time, but if the load exceeds 30 A then the fuse in the consumer unit will blow. Separate from the ring main there are usually radial circuits running from the consumer unit to supply appliances that are permanently connected and which have a high load (and therefore require a larger cable), such as a cooker, immersion heater or shower. The floor area served by a ring main should not exceed 100 m^2. A radial supply can also be taken off a ring main – this is known as a 'spur' – which can only serve one double socket outlet or one fixed appliance (served by a fused connection box).

Older properties had lighting circuits that were arranged using a junction box system, with a cable run from the fuse box to a series of junction boxes. Each junction box served a light and its switch. In modern houses, the lighting is also kept separate from the power circuit. There are usually two circuits, one for each floor, and the wiring is taken to the lights in what is known as a 'loop in' system. The cable runs from the consumer unit to each lighting rose and a cable of the same size then connects the rose to the switch. Light fittings are then connected to the ceiling rose. Lights do not consume as much power as most appliances, and the cable does not return to the consumer unit. The circuit is therefore a radial system, and is usually protected by a 5 A fuse, which will carry a load of about twelve 100 W bulbs.

Fuses

The function of a fuse is to prevent fire or heat damage in cables that are over-loaded. Fuses are located in the consumer unit, with one for each circuit in the house. Fuses are also located in some socket outlets, as well as in the plug of every moveable appliance. They are designed to fail before any serious damage occurs to the circuit and so have a current rating less than the cable or appliance they are intended to protect.

The surveyor will encounter three principal types of fuse:

• *Rewirable fuses* – still found in older houses, these consist of a piece of tinned copper wire of a diameter dependent on their current rating. They are open to abuse as the householder may replace a blown fuse with wire of a higher rating.

- *Cartridge fuses* – these consist of a wire element encased in a cartridge filled with particles of sand or a similar material. The wire element is secured to metal caps at each end. These are easier to replace and react faster than rewirable fuses. This type of fuse is also found in plugs. Cartridge fuses are colour coded to aid identification.

- *Miniature circuit breakers (MCBs)* – as provided in modern houses. A switch is turned off in the consumer unit if a fault occurs in the circuit. These are more expensive than cartridge fuses, but are more reliable and quicker to respond to a fault.

Earthing

The function of earthing is to act as a safety device to prevent electrocution. Metal parts of electrical appliances are connected to earth by means of an earth wire, to ensure that, should a live wire come into contact with a metal part, the electricity will flow through the earth wire rather than through the person holding the appliance. As this occurs, the amount of current flowing through the circuit increases, which will blow a fuse or trip an MCB. The earth terminal is normally provided by the electricity company, close to its sealed fuse.

The surveyor may encounter various methods of earthing:

- *Rising mains* – in old houses the earthing was commonly carried out using the cold water rising main. This is no longer recommended as the water main may be plastic pipework.

- *Protective multiple earthing (PME)* – this is the system used in most new houses. The neutral pole of the mains electrical supply is connected to earth at the sub-station, providing a good earth. The neutral conductor of the supply network is therefore used as the earth return path, as well as performing its normal function of carrying current. The protective metal sheath of the mains cable is connected to the earth wire.

- *Earth rods* – where the protective metal sheath of the earth wire is not continuous, or in areas where PME has not yet been implemented, earthing can be carried out using a copper stake driven into the ground. This method is not as good as PME as it is affected by the type, firmness and water content of the soil. When this method is used, a backup device is usually installed, such as an earth leakage circuit breaker.

- *Earth leakage circuit breaker (ELCB) residual current device* – similar to (but not to be confused with) MCBs, these are found in the consumer unit rather than the mains switch. They monitor the amount of current entering and leaving a circuit. If the two are not the same, the difference must have leaked to earth and the ELCB 'trips off'. ELCBs are very sensitive and their reaction time is very short.

Bonding

Any metal elements that might accidentally come into contact with an electrical current and cause electrocution need to be 'bonded' – that is, connected to the main earth terminal to create an earthed equipotential zone. Since a wet body is less resistant to shock, bonding is particularly important in bathrooms and shower rooms.

Wiring and fittings

The inspection of wiring and fittings gives the biggest clue as to the likely age and condition of the installation. The main wiring carrying the electricity supply to the outlets is referred to as a 'cable' and consists of conducting wires and protective insulation. The conducting wires are usually made of copper (sometimes aluminium is used). The rating is based on the cross-sectional area of the wires – for example, a power ring circuit may be rated as $2.5\,mm^2$. Cables with a cross-sectional area of $2.5\,mm^2$ are single-stranded, but above this size they are usually made up of multiple strands of copper. The earth conductor is slightly smaller than the other two as it only carries a load when there is a fault. Circuits carrying a heavy current, such as a cooker, have a rating of $6–10\,mm^2$.

The insulating material around the wires is usually PVC, as is the sheathing around the cable. PVC is used because it is relatively tough, incombustible and inert, and it does not deteriorate with age, although it does soften at temperatures around 70°C. PVC is suitable for burying in most plasters. Mineral-insulated, metal-sheathed cable is rarely used in housing because of its high cost. PVC cable has been used for about the past 40 years, but before this, cloth-covered, rubber insulated cable was used. The rubber was prone to perishing, leading to short circuits and possible fires. In even older (pre-Second World War) properties, lead sheathed cable may be found. The actual wires were insulated with rubber and the lead sheathing acted as an earth – there were dangers that the earthing arrangement would be compromised if the lead was damaged. Anything other than PVC-sheathed cable will have reached the end of its life, and some early PVC-cabled installations will also be nearing the ends of their lives. The IEE Wiring Regulations recommend that installations are tested every five years, and even if the surveyor's visual inspection reveals no problems this advice about regular testing should be passed on to the client.

Socket outlets have also changed over the years. Early sockets were a two-pin type – these lacked earth protection, and there were no fuses in the plugs. In the 1930s, these were replaced with round three-pin sockets – these were earthed, but the plugs still lacked fuses. The modern square-pin 13-A sockets have been used since the 1950s, but when inspecting houses it should be remembered that these might be connected to old wiring.

Cables can be laid in conduit or trunking. Conduit consists of metal or PVC tubes which protect cables from being damaged and allow cables to be withdrawn without affecting the finishes of the building. Trunking performs a similar function but provides continuous access to the cable.

It is usual to bury cables below the wall surface and this is best done by cutting a chase in the masonry so that the cable is protected by the full thickness of the plaster. Cables should only be run vertically down walls and horizontal runs should be contained in floor or ceiling voids. The following points should also be observed:

- Cabling runs in joists should be drilled a minimum of 50 mm below the surface to avoid nail damage.
- Cables should be fixed to joists where running parallel to them and should not be run diagonally across floors or ceiling, bent sharply or fixed to the top of ceiling joists in roof spaces.
- Cables passing through masonry walls should be protected by conduit.
- Contact between PVC cables and cement, polystyrene and water should be avoided.
- Cables should not be allowed to overheat – for example by being in contact with hot water cylinders. Cables can also overheat if covered with roof insulation, therefore wiring should be above and not below the insulation.

Common defects

Defects in electrical installations are obviously very serious because of the safety implications. In addition to matters raised above, the surveyor should look for the following common defects:

- Overloading the circuit by using socket adapters, which generally indicates a lack of socket outlets.
- Replacing fuse wire with wire of an incorrect rating, or with wire not intended for the purpose. (The author has witnessed a former paper-clip used as 'fuse wire' for a lighting circuit.)
- Substituting metal elements for non-metal elements without attending to earthing arrangements, such as replacing plastic switches and ceiling roses with brass ones.
- Using light switches rather than pull cords in bathrooms, where people are likely to touch the switch with a wet hand.
- Running a spur off a spur.
- Loose connections in the plug or socket. This can cause overheating and scorching.
- Using light bulbs that have too high a wattage for the light shade.
- Rodent damage to wiring.
  (Marshall and Worthing, 2006, pp 277–287).

Heating and associated installations

The inspection should identify the type, age and general condition of the heating source, including ventilation and siting requirements and flue condition where possible. The heating control system, including programmers, thermostats, valves and controllers, should be located and identified. A sample of the pipe-work, heat emitters and associated appliances (including water storage tanks) should be inspected to allow a general assessment of condition and suitability without any form of test. Any obvious hazards or safety issues associated with the heating installation should be reported.

In urban locations, the fuel most commonly used by heating appliances is mains gas, but where this is not available (and where the building owner has a prejudice against gas), oil, liquefied petroleum gas or solid fuel may be used. Alternatively, off-peak electrical heating may be installed.

Wet heating systems

A visual inspection of the boiler should be carried out and an estimate of its age made. In many cases, a history of recent service work is attached either to the boiler itself or to a nearby position. If there is no evidence of a recent service having been carried out then the client should be advised of this fact. Ventilation arrangements for conventional flued heating appliances should be checked. There should be a permanent ventilation opening, of at least the same size as the flue, provided close to the boiler. Where the appliance has a balanced flue the surveyor should check that this is no closer than 600 mm to a window or door and that it is guarded and is not obstructed (e.g. by vegetation). The proximity of combustible material to the balanced flue should also be checked – it is not uncommon for the flue to be located too close to PVC rainwater goods, causing them to deform. A heat shield should be provided if the flue is closer than 1 m from combustible material.

The type of heating system should then be ascertained – that is, is it a vented or unvented system? The latter operates at mains pressure and there will be no feed and expansion (or header) tank, which in a vented system is usually located in the roof space. Building Regulations and water by-laws have only permitted unvented systems in the UK since 1986, and such systems must have been installed by a British Board of Agrément certified contractor. Safety devices, including an expansion vessel, are required with an unvented system, and in hard water areas the surveyor will need to check that a water softener is provided to prevent furring of the boiler.

Modern wet central heating systems (whether vented or unvented) all have both a flow pipe and a return pipe connecting the boiler to the radiators, but older systems may only have a single pipe acting as flow and return. The one-pipe system was fairly common in houses built during the 1960s and 1970s, and the author has recently inspected a house that still has its original one-pipe system. The obvious disadvantage of such as system is that the radiators closest to the boiler will be much warmer than the ones furthest away. If both flow and return valves are connected to the same pipe then the system is a one-pipe type.

The use of microbore pipework has become quite common in recent years, particularly in refurbishment work where there is limited space to accommodate the usual 15–22-mm diameter flow and return pipework. Such a system uses a manifold which has traditional-sized flow and return pipes running between it and the boiler, but which has 8, 10 or 12-mm diameter pipes running from it to the radiators. The use of special double-entry valves at one side of the radiator only is fairly common with microbore installations. The disadvantages of such installations are that the smaller and softer pipes are more prone to blockage and are more easily damaged.

When inspecting a wet central heating system:

- The heating system should be switched on – even if the inspection is carried out in the middle of summer. Obviously, the owner's consent is required to use the fuel that they are paying for and there must be fuel available. If for any reason it is not possible to operate the heating system then the client should be advised of this fact. It will be appreciated that the radiators will take some time to heat up and so this element of the inspection should not be left until the end of the visit.
- All radiators should be checked to ensure they are warm.
- Valves should be turned to make sure that they are not stuck – most modern systems have thermostatically controlled valves and if these do not operate then it will not be possible to control the system.
- Evidence of corrosion to radiators should be looked for, as well as possible leaks. The presence of cold spots at the tops of radiators suggests air locks and the client should be advised that the system requires bleeding. However, cold spots at the bottoms of radiators suggest that there is sludge in the radiators. This is caused by corrosion within the system resulting from air gaining entry, and remedial work including the removal of the sludge and the use of a corrosion inhibitor within the header tank should be advised.
- The header tank should be inspected for the existence of a cover, insulation and an overflow pipe. Most modern tanks will be plastic, but if the tank is an old galvanised steel or asbestos type the client should be advised that it requires replacement.
- All pipework associated with the heating system should be lagged where it is located in unheated areas of the building.

When inspecting dry heating systems there is little that can be checked, particularly if the inspection is carried out in the summer months when the installation is not in operation. Since such systems generally use off-peak electricity, the surveyor will not be able to switch the system on. In such cases, all that the surveyor can do is comment on the age of the electric storage heaters, etc. Some electric warm air heating systems were installed in the 1960s or 1970s, but very few remain since the cost of operating such systems proved excessively high.

Plumbing installations

As well as noting whether the property has a mains or private supply, an assessment should be made of whether the provision is suitable within the context of the type of property and its location. The stopcock should be located and a sample of the pipework, control valves, water storage tanks and associated appliances and fixtures should be inspected, but not tested. Kitchen and sanitary fittings should be inspected to assess their general condition. Any obvious hazards or safety issues associated with the plumbing installation should be noted.

Water supply

If there is a private supply then laboratory testing of the water should be recommended. The type of cold-water installation should be ascertained – it will either be direct off the mains or indirect (incorporating a cold water storage cistern, probably located in the roof space). The obvious disadvantage of a direct supply is that there are no storage facilities available should the mains supply be disconnected.

The stopcock will probably be located beneath the kitchen sink in a modern property, but in a pre-war property it may be located in an understairs cupboard, or even beneath a ground floor floorboard (usually just inside the front door). In some even older properties the stopcock may be located outside the house, in a box in the garden or under the front path.

The material of the rising main should be identified. In most modern properties the pipework will be of polythene, but in older properties it may be in lead, in which case the health hazards should be advised to the client. The stopcock should be operated to ensure that it does disconnect the supply of water to the property.

See also: Environmental issues, page 91

Hot and cold water storage

The position of the cold water storage cistern should be located and its type and condition ascertained. In most cases, the tank is to be found in the roof space –

the method of support should be checked to ensure that the roof structure is not being overloaded. If the tank is of asbestos cement or galvanised steel then its replacement should be recommended. Lagging of the tank and pipework should be verified, together with the presence of a cover and overflow. The roof insulation should not be carried under the cistern.

The hot water storage tank or cylinder should be located and its type noted. The presence of any electric immersion heaters should be recorded. Most modern cylinders have two heaters fitted, one connected to the off-peak supply (for use during the summer months when hot water for heating is not required) and the other connected to the normal supply for boost purposes only. Off-peak electricity is the least expensive method of heating hot water when the boiler is not being used for central heating. An insulation jacket of at least 80 mm thickness should be provided and the presence of a thermostat should be verified.

The type of hot and cold water distribution pipework should be noted. In most cases it will be copper, but plastic pipework is increasingly being used in new houses. If there is any lead pipework present then the client should be advised to replace this as soon as possible.

Fittings

The type, location and general condition of kitchen and sanitary fittings should be noted. If the kitchen units are the cheapest self-assembly type then the client must not be left under the impression that they are of the highest quality. Sanitary fittings should be carefully inspected to ensure that they are not chipped or cracked – are the WC seats attached to the pans? Mechanical ventilation of bathrooms and kitchens should be checked. Leaks from sanitary fittings should be looked for and all the WC cisterns should be checked to ensure they have an overflow properly connected.

Underground drainage systems

The type of underground drainage installation and sewerage disposal system should be identified and an assessment made of its general suitability within the context of the type of property and its location. Inspection chambers, cesspits and septic tanks should be located, and light and accessible covers should be raised so that these can be inspected internally and their suitability assessed.

The routes of the underground drain runs should be located where possible and any potential defects recorded, but without any specialist tests. The suitability and condition of visible gullies should be recorded.

The drainage will be connected to one of four types of system:

- *separate foul and combined sewers* – most usual in modern developments, particularly in urban locations
- *foul water sewer with surface water to soakaways* – mainly found in semi-rural locations (there is a variation of this system, where surface water at the front of the property drains to the surface water sewer serving the road, but where there are soakaways at the rear)
- *combined foul and surface water sewers* – common in urban locations, particularly older properties
- *private treatment installation (cess pit or septic tank)* – found in rural locations where no mains drainage is available.

The surveyor should raise any inspection chamber cover that can be raised by one person with reasonable effort and run water through the system(s) to ensure that no blockages are evident. The location and severity of any blockages should be recorded. The position of any solids within the system should also be noted. From the condition of the drains visible within the chambers, an assessment should be made of the likely age of the system and whether it has been renewed since the construction of the building. If the jointing between channels in the chamber is in poor condition then it is possible that the joints between sections of drain are in a similar condition. Where alterations have been made, have branches been connected at benching level? It is much easier for the builder to connect new branches at a higher level, but this will probably lead to blockages. If the walls of the interior of the chamber are rendered, the condition of the rendering should be noted. It was common to fit interceptor traps to the chamber nearest the sewer, but such traps are often the cause of blockages. If such a trap is fitted, the presence of the cover to the rodding eye should be noted – if the cover is missing, rats can enter the drains of the property.

Cesspits are tanks that have sufficient capacity to store a minimum of 45 days' effluent, and which therefore require emptying several times a year – at an annual cost of several thousands of pounds. Septic tanks, on the other hand, treat the effluent by biological action before the 'clean' water is disposed of to a water course or a soakaway. The permission of the National Rivers Authority is required for this discharge, and in certain sensitive environmental areas (such as in parts of the Norfolk Broads) such discharge is not permitted – a full scale private treatment works is then required. It is recommended that a septic tank is desludged every six months. Older tanks usually consist of two brick chambers, but modern tanks consist of an onion-shaped glass-reinforced plastic vessel. It is impossible from a simple visual inspection to determine whether either a cesspit or a septic tank is operating satisfactorily, and one family's production of effluent may be very different from another's. When inspecting private treatment installations, the client should always be advised that it is only possible to assess the efficiency of a private installation through use over a period of time.

It is usually impossible to locate surface water soakaways, unless they have caused some settlement of the garden above them. They should be sited at least 4.5 m from any building. Usually, rainwater downpipes are not provided with gullies when they are connected to soakaways, so the only way to carry out any form of water runaway test is from a paving gulley. Rainwater downpipes must be connected to a gulley if the drainage installation is of a combined type.

As well as inspecting those parts of the system to which access is available, it will be necessary to assess the likely condition of other parts of the drainage system. Where there is cracking to adjacent walls and/or pavings or where there has been

See also: Contractors, page 30

some settlement of pavings then leaking drains are a possible cause. If there is any doubt about the watertightness of the installation then a test should be recommended.

Above ground drainage and rainwater systems

The type of above ground drainage installation (including guttering and rain-water pipes) should be recorded and an assessment made of its suitability for the type of property. The main stack pipe should be located, as well as branch connections and other associated fittings and appliances, and an assessment made of their suitability, but without any special tests. The condition of visible waste traps and fittings and appliances should be recorded and an assessment made of the condition of visible gutters and rainwater downpipes.

The two-pipe plumbing system will generally be found in houses dating from the 1920s until the 1950s, provided that this has not been updated. One pipe carries the soil water from the WC and the other carries the waste water from the bath and basin. On many houses the waste pipe also carries water from the roof. The system worked well as the combination of waste and rainwater flushed the system. However, a weak point is the hopper head, which can become blocked with waste products and leaves, and this should be checked (it is usually possible to do this from the bathroom window).

The one-pipe system was introduced during the 1950s as a result of design work by the BRE. A single stack carries soil and waste water, but to prevent trap sypho-nage there are restrictions on the length and gradient of branch drain runs, which the surveyor should check:

- bath and sink: maximum branch drain length is 3 m for a 40 mm pipe, slope 18–90 mm depending on length
- wash basin: maximum length 1.7 m for a 32 mm pipe
- WC: 6 m maximum for 100 mm pipe, minimum slope of 18 mm per m.

In addition, where the waste branch is below the WC branch, it should be a minimum of 200 mm below to prevent WC soil water backing up the waste branch. The distance between the lowest connection and the drain invert must be at least 450 mm, otherwise the fitting must be connected to the below ground drainage system. There must be a large radius bend to connect the stack to the drain, and the top of the stack must vent to the external air and be well clear of any window opening. The alternative is to provide an air admit-tance valve at the top of the pipe. This allows air in but will not allow any air (and therefore smells) out, and may be located in, for example, the roof space. Single stacks can be used externally on buildings of up to three storeys high, but above this height the stack must be located internally – so that easy access to it is available. On commercial buildings where the design criteria of the single-stack system cannot be met, the surveyor should expect to find a separate ventilation system to ensure that trap syphonage does not occur.

When inspecting above ground drainage, the essential matters to be checked are:

- signs of leaks
- adequate support of branch drains.

When inspecting rainwater goods during dry weather, indications of leaks should be looked for. Very often, white and green staining will be evident on the under-side of gutters, especially at joints, where they are not watertight, and there may be staining on paving immediately beneath the guttering. Downpipes should be checked for any sign of blockage or leakage, paying particular attention to the rear of the pipe. Most modern rainwater goods are plastic and the support of gutters in particular should be checked. Cast iron rainwater goods should be checked for any sign of corrosion, and downpipes should be tapped with a small metal object. If they are watertight there is a high-pitched note, but a much duller or deader sound is heard if they are not. It is also often possible to hear rust falling down the inside of the pipe when carrying out this operation. During the period when cast iron rainwater goods were being replaced with plastic items, asbestos cement rainwater goods were sometimes used. The joints of any remaining asbestos cement gutters are unlikely to be watertight – the material is very brittle and susceptible to impact damage, and there are of course health problems associated with asbestos.

Gas installations and oil storage

The gas or oil supply (e.g. natural gas supply, or liquefied petroleum gas or heating oil tank) should be ascertained and its suitability assessed. The bulk storage container, gas meter and control valve should be located and their suitability assessed. A sample of pipework, the control valves and any associated appliances should be inspected for condition, presence of ventilation and suitability, but without any special tests. Any obvious hazards or safety issues associated with the installation should be identified.

Where gas is used, the position of the gas meter should be located and noted. Where fuel is stored then the receptacle should be inspected and its condition noted. Most oil storage tanks are now plastic, but where an old steel tank remains, it should be carefully inspected for corrosion, paying particular attention to the underside. The level of oil or gas in a tank should be recorded.

Other services

Where fire alarms, security installations, CCTV, or other services exist, these should be located and identified. Perhaps the most common item to be inspected is the security system, but for obvious reasons most owners are averse to actually demonstrating this. If this is the case then the client should be advised accordingly. However, basic details such as the location of sensors and whether the system is linked to any external monitoring system should be noted.

Environmental issues

The surveyor should inspect for visual signs of contamination by harmful substances, but should not research the presence or possible consequences of these factors. Typical contaminants in this context include asbestos, high-voltage electricity supply equipment, lead, mining (in known mining areas a mining search is recommended), proximity to landfill sites and proximity to chemical or other plants producing noxious or unpleasant smells.

In areas of high incidence of radon gas, it would be appropriate for the surveyor to advise that radon measurements and remedial measures might be required (see Dixon and Scivyer, 1999, for guidance from the National Radiological Protection Board and the BRE on the measurement of radon and remedial measures).

If asbestos products are identified, an assessment will be required of what risk these present. In general, loose fibrous materials such as lagging present far more of a risk than asbestos cement components in good condition. If in doubt, it is best to advise that specialist advice is sought, and that if removal is required then this must be undertaken by a licensed contractor.

Recent studies have indicated that there is a slightly increased risk of certain cancers in children living close to overhead power cables. If the property is located close to such power lines then the client must be advised of the slight potential risk. Similarly, there is also a slight risk if the property is close to a landfill site.

As indicated previously, because of the dangers of lead poisoning, the client should be advised to remove any lead plumbing. Where, however, the water main is still in lead pipework then the recommendation should be that the Water Company is asked to measure the lead content of the water. If this is high then the company has a duty to replace the water main up to the customer's stopcock.

If the surveyor suspects that the building has been built on, or is close to, contaminated land then the client should be advised that this could have a serious impact on the value of the property. Of course, if the surveyor is unaware of the contaminated land then they are at a serious disadvantage. This is yet another reason for the advice given previously, that surveyors should only survey buildings in geographical areas with which they are familiar.

See also:
Location,
page 105
Potential to flood is becoming of increasing concern to surveyors as a result of global warming.

Insulation

Both thermal insulation and sound insulation should be considered. The surveyor should identify so far as is possible the levels of thermal insulation in the building. This will normally include roof and wall insulation, double glazing, floor insulation, draughtproofing and insulation to plumbing, heating pipes and tanks. Obviously, the extent of this inspection will often be restricted as much insulation in a building is concealed within the construction.

Any divergence from good levels of thermal insulation should be reported to the client. The extent of this element of a survey obviously overlaps with the gathering of the data required to compile an Energy Performance Certificate – indeed, the surveyor may well have been instructed to provide both services (provided of course that they are qualified as an energy assessor).

In terms of sound insulation, there is a requirement to check for insulation between neighbouring properties and insulation to the external walls and windows. Again, the extent of this inspection will often be restricted, as much insulation will be concealed within the construction. Obviously, this element only applies to buildings that are linked vertically or horizontally to another. In modern properties the levels of insulation are likely to be good, but in older dwellings they may be very poor. In one town in which the author has practised it was not uncommon for the party wall between terraced houses to be only half a brick thick. This thickness of brickwork obviously provides very poor sound insulation. If there is any concern about levels of insulation then it would be appropriate to advise that a building services engineer carry out acoustic tests – although, of course, the adjoining owner would need to consent to these tests. If the building is in an area where high noise levels are encountered, this should always be pointed out to the client – just in case they had not noticed!

SUMMARY

- At present, the UK surveyor is only required to inspect service installations and not to test them. If we are to follow the example of US Home Inspectors then this may change at some time in the future.
- The surveyor must be extremely thorough in the inspection of the electrical, plumbing and drainage installations and in the assessment of environmental matters.
- The surveyor should be able to recognise old electrical fittings and wiring and should recommend a test of the installation where there is concern about its age.
- When inspecting plumbing and heating systems it is necessary to locate and report on the mains water stopcock, storage cisterns, boilers and hot water storage cylinders. If there are concerns about the age and condition of any appliance then these should be reported to the client.
- Central heating systems should be operated where possible (obviously, if mains services are not connected, this will not be possible).
- Covers of drainage inspection chambers should be raised, and wherever possible water should be run through the system(s).
- Any environmental concerns, such as potential to flood, high levels of radon in the area, overhead power cables and asbestos, should be noted.
- The levels of insulation should be noted and reported on, including cross-referencing to the Energy Performance Certificate.

Section 9
What to inspect – other elements

In this Section:

- *External joinery and decorations*
- *Internal walls and partitions*
- *Floors and ceilings*
- *Staircases*
- *Internal doors*
- *Fireplaces and chimney stacks*
- *Unwelcome visitors*
- *Site, boundaries and outbuildings*
- *Location*
- *Non-standard construction*

Introduction

The elements of a survey that result in most negligence claims have been considered in Section 7, followed by services and environmental matters in Section 8. The secondary or slightly less 'risky' items are considered in this section. It will be appreciated, however, that these items still require the same degree of professional care when carrying out the inspection. The main things to be aware of when undertaking the inspection of these secondary elements are discussed below.

External joinery and decorations

Wet rot has been considered in Section 7, and where there is painted softwood external joinery this is the main concern. However, hardwood, plastic and metal

See also:
Fungal attack,
page 68

frames also require careful inspection. Even where there are non-softwood windows and doors there may be softwood roof fascia, soffit and barge boards. These will require careful inspection, including probing at susceptible locations, such as the bottom of barge boards. Where such locations are beyond the reach of the standard length of a surveyor's ladder then inspection should be made using binoculars. These comments also apply to any horizontal or vertical timber cladding to walls.

Many metal windows such as those manufactured by the Essex-based company Crittal are still in existence, particularly in local authority houses built during the 1950s and 1960s. Common problems with these are distorted frames and excessive condensation. Some sliding aluminium windows installed in houses built in the 1970s have poor serviceability, and because they were only single glazed, they suffer from condensation. All casements and sashes should be checked to ensure that they open and close satisfactorily. The fashion for uPVC replacement windows shows little sign of abating, and when inspecting these the following should be considered:

- Are the product and installation of good quality?
- Is an insurance-backed guarantee available?
- Is adequate natural light and ventilation provided to habitable rooms?

All double glazed sealed units should be checked to ensure that no condensation is occurring between the panes as a result of defective edge seals. Most good-quality double glazed sealed units have a ten-year guarantee.

Security should also be considered when inspecting windows and external walls. The adequacy of window locks and the existence of mortice deadlocks to doors should be checked.

The estimated life to the next external redecoration should be noted. Any onerous maintenance liabilities such as extensive areas of painted walls or cladding should be recorded.

Internal walls and partitions

By examining the layout of upper floor walls, floor joist directions and any intermediate support to the roof structure, the surveyor should determine which internal walls are loadbearing. Structural problems only affecting the internal walls are not uncommon, particularly in pre-Second World War properties where foundations to internal walls were frequently shallower and less substantial than those to the external walls. In addition, where floor joists run front to rear and a roof purlin also struts onto the main cross wall, this wall carries twice the vertical loads imposed on the external walls. As mentioned in Section 7, clients of the author awoke one night to discover that their bed was sliding across the upper floor bedroom. A water main beneath the sand subsoil had burst, causing the foundation to the main cross wall to subside. This resulted in extensive damage to the partition itself and to the floor and roof structures that it supported. Sloping floors and distorted door openings are indications of less significant but still serious structural movement of loadbearing internal walls. A spirit level should be used to check for these telltale signs. Internal door openings should be inspected carefully by opening and closing all doors, and any signs of recent easing of doors should be noted.

Some 20 years ago there was a fashion in new speculative housing for supporting concrete blockwork partitions off doubled-up timber floor joists. While it was possible to prove by calculation that the timber beam was capable of carrying the load, sometimes excessive drying shrinkage of the joists caused significant deflection to occur. This defect very often manifests itself as cracking between the first floor partition and the ceiling and with some distortion of adjacent door openings.

Another method of construction that has become fashionable in speculative housing over the past 20 years is the use of very lightweight plasterboard partitions in non-loadbearing situations. Clients purchasing such properties should be informed of this type of partition's relatively poor sound insulation, low impact-damage resistance and inability to support heavy fixings.

The state of internal decoration should be recorded and a general comment provided in the report. It will be appreciated that many purchasers prefer to completely redecorate their new property. However, any dangerous materials (such as polystyrene ceiling tiles) or possibly expensive to replace decorations (such as textured wall finishes) should be reported on.

Floors

The most serious defects likely to affect suspended timber ground and first floors (fungal attack and insect infestation) have been considered in Section 7. The importance of checking for adequate sub-floor ventilation in suspended timber ground floors cannot be emphasised enough. In most older properties, the current Building Regulations' requirement of one 225 × 150 mm airbrick every 1,500 mm is unlikely to be satisfied. What should be looked for is a sufficient number of airbricks to ensure a through flow of air beneath the floor. Where extensions with solid floors have been built at the rear of properties with suspended timber ground floors, evidence of ducting to adequately vent what is now an internal floor void should be looked for.

It is necessary to raise one floorboard at each floor level in order to assess conditions within the sub-floor void. Fixed boards should be raised for a full building survey, but the surveyor is only required to raise loose boards when undertaking the intermediate level inspection. In most Victorian and Edwardian properties there is a loose floor board where the cold water rising main enters, usually just inside the front door or in the understairs cupboard, and this is the most convenient position at which to inspect the ground floor void (with the aid of a small mirror and a torch). The existence of a concrete subfloor, any build-up of debris or dampness in the void, adequate honeycombing of sleeper walls and the presence of damp-proof courses (DPCs) between wall plate and sleeper wall can usually be checked by an inspection from a single point.

All suspended timber floors should be checked for excessive deflection by bouncing up and down on them. Where there is excessive deflection then problems should be anticipated and further investigation should be recommended.

Solid ground floors should be checked for signs of settlement or heave. Heave may be the result of sulphate attack, or may be caused by swelling of hardcore additives or a clay subsoil (usually following removal of vegetation).

See also:
Trees, page 61

Settlement is usually caused by failure to compact the hardcore adequately or by subsidence of the subsoil. Table 9.1, reproduced from BRE Digest 251, indicates the typical signs of a solid concrete floor suffering from settlement and provides a method of classifying the damage caused. The main signs of a heaving floor are doors catching on the floor and a clear rise in the level of the floor slab at some point. In extreme cases, the external walls are pushed outwards by the swelling floor and there is slippage of the walls at DPC level.

The other main concern with a ground floor solid floor is the adequacy of the damp-proof membrane. A moisture meter is essential for the determination of any damp defects, and readings should be obtained not only from the floor

TABLE 9.1: *Classification of visible damage caused by ground floor slab settlement*

Damage category	Description of typical damage	Approximate (a) crack width (b) gap*
0	Hairline cracks between floor and skirtings.	(a) NA (b) Up to 1 mm
1	Settlement of the floor slab, either at a corner or along a short wall, or possibly uniformly, such that a gap opens up below skirting boards which can be masked by resetting skirting boards. No cracks in walls. No cracks in floor slab, although there may be negligible cracks in floor screed and finish. Slab reasonably level.	(a) NA (b) Up to 6 mm
2	Larger gaps below skirting boards, some obvious but limited local settlement leading to a slight slope of floor slab; gaps can be masked by resetting skirting boards and some local rescreeding may be necessary. Fine cracks appear in internal partition walls which need some redecoration; slight distortion in door frames so some 'jamming' may occur, necessitating adjustment of doors. No cracks in floor slab although there may be very slight cracks in floor screed and finish. Slab reasonably level.	(a) Up to 1 mm (b) Up to 13 mm
3	Significant gaps below skirting boards with areas of floor, especially at corners or ends, where local settlements may have caused slight cracking of floor slab. Sloping of floor in these areas is clearly visible (slope approximately 1 in 150). Some disruption to drain, plumbing or heating pipes may occur. Damage to internal walls is more widespread with some crack filling or replastering of partitions necessary. Doors may have to be refitted. Inspection reveals some voids below slab with poor or loosely compacted fill.	(a) Up to 5 mm (b) Up to 19 mm
4	Large, localised gaps below skirting boards; possibly some cracks in floor slab with sharp fall to edge of slab (slope approximately 1 in 500 or more). Inspection reveals voids exceeding 50 mm below slab and/or poor or loose fill likely to settle further. Local breaking-out, part refilling and relaying of floor slab or grouting of fill may be necessary; damage to internal partitions may require replacement of some bricks or blocks or relining of stud partitions.	(a) 5 to 15 mm but may also depend on number of cracks (b) Up to 25 mm
5	Either very large, overall floor settlement with large movement of walls and damage at junctions extending up to 1st floor area, with possible damage to exterior walls, or large differential settlements across floor slab. Voids exceeding 75 mm below slab and/or very poor or very loose fill likely to settle further. Risk of instability. Most or all of floor slab requires breaking out and relaying or grouting of fill; internal partitions need replacement.	(a) Usually greater than 15 mm but depends on number of cracks (b) Greater than 25 mm

* 'Gap' refers to space – usually between the skirting and finished floor – caused by settlement after making appropriate allowance for discrepancy in building, shrinkage, normal bedding and the like.

Source: Copyright BRE (1995), reproduced from BRE Digest 251 with permission.

surface, but also from skirting boards and the wall plaster immediately above skirting board level.

The main concern with suspended timber upper floors apart from woodworm infestation is their structural adequacy. In poorer quality speculative housing of the Georgian and later periods, very slender joists were sometimes used – particularly in rear additions – and these are prone to deflection and in a few cases total failure. Again, the main way to test all suspended timber floors is to jump up and down on them.

Suspended concrete floor slabs will be encountered in some properties built during the second half of the 20th century, particularly in blocks of flats. Structural problems with such floors are not common, but the surveyor should be alert to the possible use of high alumina cement (HAC) in their construction if built before the mid 1970s. Concrete containing HAC can deteriorate rapidly (and in extreme cases fail) in warm and humid conditions. See Dunster and Holton (2000) for the latest BRE guidance on the assessment of ageing HAC concrete.

Ceilings

While some assessment of the condition of ceilings is possible from an inspection of their underside, it is only possible to determine the type (and therefore the potential problems with) the ceiling following an inspection from above. On the top floor this can obviously be accomplished from within the roof space, but at lower floor levels it is necessary to raise a floorboard. In domestic situations the material used for ceilings since the interwar period is, of course, plasterboard. Generally, this material suffers little from defects unless it becomes wet. If affected by roof or plumbing leaks, plasterboard is likely to require replacement. Of course, the material will not support very much weight from above and any excessive storage in roof spaces should be noted and reported on. Other potential problems are associated with poor quality workmanship. The lack of noggings at joints between boards, the use of nails that are too short and the use of board of inadequate thickness can all lead to problems. A client of the author's required the complete replacement of the ceiling of his new bungalow after the builder had tried to save money by using 9 mm plasterboard (instead of the 12 mm board specified) to span between trussed rafters spaced 600 mm apart.

Before the introduction of plasterboard the most common type of ceiling was lath and plaster – three coats of lime plaster applied to thin strips of softwood. Such ceilings are prone to failure as a result of the plaster losing key, rot or insect attack to the laths and water damage. Any property discovered to have lath and plaster ceilings is likely to require new ceilings in the near future. Indications of imminent failure are ceilings that are bulging or excessively cracked.

The author practised for many years in an area close to the Norfolk Broads and in this area it was common to find reed and plaster ceilings. These suffer from similar problems to lath and plaster ceilings and generally have a shorter life expectancy.

Staircases

The condition of both the staircase itself (i.e. treads, risers and strings) and the balustrades and handrails should be inspected. Woodworm infestation of older staircases is quite common and rot should be checked for where the stairs adjoin an external wall. The full requirements of the current Building Regulations are unlikely to be complied with in older staircases, but any design issue that is seriously short of modern standards will need to be commented on. If, for example, the headroom over one flight is low then a tall client is likely to take exception if this fact has not been pointed out in the survey report. Items that impact on safety, such as narrow winding treads or balustrades with ranch-style bars or with any large openings, should be particularly highlighted.

Internal doors

The type of door in each room should be recorded together with a note of its condition. As indicated above, every door should be opened and closed. Particular attention should be paid to the head of the opening as any distortion in this position is a likely indication of structural movement. Attention should also be paid to the bottoms of the doors to ensure that there are no excessive gaps – in one bungalow the author inspected the internal doors had 50 mm gaps beneath them! The condition of ironmongery should be recorded.

In properties requiring fire certification, many doors will have to be fire doors (this also applies in some domestic situations – for example, between an integral garage and the dwelling). When inspecting fire doors, the operation of door closers should be checked and the depths of rebates should be verified.

Fireplaces and chimney stacks

Great care is required when inspecting any property that has chimney stacks, and the surveyor should ensure that sufficient time is allowed to inspect fully all aspects of the stacks. The difficulty, of course, is that the various components of each stack are to be found in several different locations, and that missing one small piece of evidence can lead to errors. When inspecting the exterior, the number and locations of stacks should be recorded (it can be useful to do this by drawing them on the roof plan that is drawn during the early stages of the inspection). The number of flues should be recorded together with the condition of the brickwork and flashings. The folly of rendering brick chimney stacks above roof level should be reported to the client if appropriate.

See also: Arriving on site, page 43

The next careful inspection required is in the roof space, where the existence of the chimneys should be verified and a note of the condition recorded, paying particular attention to any evidence of rain penetration (with the aid of a moisture meter). It is common for the builder to have engraved the date of construction into the rendering of the stack in a roof space, which may be helpful information for the surveyor. Any support of chimney breast brickwork at or just above the upper floor level should be noted.

Then, the existence of the chimney breast should be verified in each room. Where the chimney breast is missing, the method of support should be ascertained, as far as this is possible. If any brickwork is supported off ceiling or floor joists then the need for additional support, using steelwork, should be reported to the client.

Where flues are no longer used then ventilation of these should be verified (or recommended where it is missing). Where fireplaces are evident, the flue should be inspected with the aid of a small mirror and a torch. Where brick flues are not lined then the possible need for lining in the future should be reported. Where a conventional flued heating appliance makes use of any chimney stack flue then an appropriately sited ventilation opening of at least the size of the flue should be checked for and recommended if missing. The existence of a standard flue liner terminal at roof level suggests that the flue has been lined, but is not certain evidence that the flue has been satisfactorily lined. Where there is a statutory need for monitoring of heating appliances (such as in houses in multiple occupation), a carbon monoxide test should be carried out or recommended.

Particular care should be taken to record any evidence of dampness to chimney breasts. However, the diagnosis of the causes of such dampness is not always straightforward. Sometimes the dampness is the result of a defective flashing, but the dampness can also be coming from within the flue, either because of condensation of flue gases or as a result of rain penetration (sometimes soot deposits in the flue can exaggerate the latter problem). It can take some time and expense to remedy chimney stack dampness problems and the client should be put on notice of this fact.

Unwelcome visitors

Humans are not the only creatures who will take up occupation of buildings given half a chance – there are innumerable unwelcome visitors that the surveyor must be alert to discovering and advising the client about. Where dogs and cats also occupy dwellings then it is possible that fleas will also take up residence. In hot weather, a few fleas can quickly turn into an epidemic. The new owner would need to fumigate all carpets before taking up occupation.

Even if the surveyor does not see any evidence of rats or mice, they may see traps that have been left for these rodents – particularly in roof spaces. The surveyor should then report that rodents have probably been a problem in the past. Squirrels will also enter buildings, particularly when looking for somewhere to hibernate.

Bats are protected by statute, and if encountered (usually in the roof space) should not be disturbed. Piles of droppings and discarded insect wings are usually the first signs of the presence of bats in a roof space. Any woodworm or rot eradication treatments necessary to the roof timbers would need to be those which do not affect bats.

The final 'inhabitants' to be included in this section may seem rather strange, and there is certainly no known method of detecting them – ghosts. Whether the surveyor, author or indeed the reader believes in such phenomena is not at issue here, but what is certain is that some people believe certain properties to be haunted. It has been shown that belief that a property is occupied by a ghost, particularly if the belief becomes widespread, can have an effect on value. Investigations by a colleague of the author have suggested that while this can have an adverse effect on domestic property values, some commercial properties such as hotels and public houses can actually have their value enhanced.

Site and boundaries

This section of the inspection should not be rushed, even though it may be carried out towards the end of the time on site. The general condition of boundary walls and fences as well as details of any significant changes in level and, in particular, the presence of retaining walls will need to be recorded. Unusual excavation features such as ha-ha trenches cannot always be spotted from ground level and so it will be necessary to inspect the site fully, unless the surveyor's instructions preclude this aspect of the inspection. Assuming they do not, then the following will need to be inspected:

- *Boundary walls* – record the construction and general condition. Very often the failure to provide thermal movement joints in masonry walls causes cracking. High brick walls can become a grave danger if they deteriorate to such an extent that they are likely to collapse. Free-standing brick arches are a particular problem and several injuries occur each year (some fatal) as a result of the collapse of such features. Even relatively new arches can be affected, particularly if there is a heavy gate constantly slamming into the supports of the arch.
- *Retaining walls* – these may be within the property or on the boundary, but in either event they should be inspected very carefully for any signs of deterioration. The existence of adequate drainage through the wall should be checked to ensure that they are not likely to collapse under waterlogged conditions (sometimes there will be land drainage, which is less easily detected).
- *Fences* – the condition of these should be noted. Generally, timber panel fences with concrete posts and gravel boards have a significant lifespan, but those fixed to timber posts have a much shorter life. Older timber fences are likely to require replacement in the near future. Chain-link and wire-stand fences obviously provide less privacy. Any fences that are not animal proof should be reported to the client. As indicated in Section 3, the solicitor will usually advise the client about the responsibility for the maintenance of the boundaries. Rules of thumb about who is responsible for a particular fence based on which side of the fence the posts are located are unreliable and should be ignored.

See also: Solicitor, page 24

- *Hedges* – without some additional fencing these may not be animal proof. The maintenance liability of hedges should be stressed in the report.
- *Trees* – the problems of trees in close proximity to buildings have been discussed in Section 7. If there are any large trees or hedges (or any that have

the potential to become large), these should be noted. As indicated previously, it is recommended that a swatch book of tree leaves be carried to aid identification.

See also:
Trees, page 61

- *Pavings* – the construction, condition (any unevenness or cracking) and approximate age of all pavings should be recorded. Asphalt drives in particular can cause problems – what can appear to be a recently paved drive at the time of inspection can deteriorate rapidly if it has been laid poorly. The temporary nature and maintenance liability of pea-shingle and gravel drives should be commented on in the report. Drainage arrangements for hard pavings should be considered – it may not be raining when the survey is carried out. In period terraces, the steps leading to the front door can often form part of the weather-protection for part of the cellar (sometimes originally used as a coal store). As these age they deteriorate, and this may lead to dampness problems in the basement.

Outbuildings

Outbuildings will not be inspected to quite the same level of detail as the main building, but it is important that any serious defects are recorded – particularly to the garage. A structure housing what may be a very expensive vehicle is expected by many clients to be in a similar condition to the main building. Yet the garage is something that clients frequently look at only very superficially when viewing a property and it is up to the surveyor to advise them whether, for instance, the flat roof requires recovering or whether the overhead door will not actually open. Other outbuildings are very often poorly maintained and the necessary advice for placing such structures back into good condition should be provided by the surveyor. The cost of demolition and reinstatement of outbuildings should be included in a fire insurance valuation.

Location

The surveyor should make a note of the general character of the locality as well as any adjoining uses that could cause nuisance to the owner (not forgetting busy roads, adjacent railway lines or overhead flight paths). An aspect that has become much more important in recent years is the potential to flood. Flooding from rivers and inundated drainage systems has increased significantly as a result of global warming and increased building on flood-plains. Any obvious hazards should be noted along with any sign of recent flood protection measures. If flooding is a potential problem then it would be appropriate to recommend that a specialist flood search be commissioned by the conveyancer.

Non-standard construction

This section is principally applicable to housing, but it also has some relevance to commercial buildings. The vast majority of houses in the UK are of traditional masonry construction, but in the interwar period and immediately after the Second World War a variety of system-built houses were constructed, and timber-framed houses became increasingly common during the second half of the 20th century. The identification of these 'non-standard' methods of construction is essential when carrying out any type of survey. This is because certain types of non-standard houses are considered unsuitable for mortgage lending by the financial institutions. This obviously affects their market value.

The surveyor will quickly become familiar with the various types of non-standard houses built in their area – most of these will have been built by local authorities, but many may now be privately owned. Generally, all brick- and tile-clad timber-framed houses are suitable for mortgage lending, except those where the 'cavity' has been filled with insulation after construction. Typical defects with timber-framed houses are largely due to poor site practice, and have been identified as follows:

- *Omission of the vapour barrier* – this should be at least 500 gauge polythene or equivalent and must be fixed to the warm side of the insulation. Fixing should be delayed until the frame has a moisture content of 20 per cent or less. Any holes for services should be neatly cut and all tears repaired with special tape.
- *Excessive notching and cutting of studs* – any cutting of the structural members to receive services should have been kept to a minimum and carried out in accordance with the recommendations of the designer of the frame.
- *Inaccurate base structure* – it is important that the base structure is 'square' to avoid any problems of frame assembly and fixing. This could result in the cavity between the frame and the cladding becoming too small, increasing the risk of rain penetration. If the base is not level, minor inaccuracies could be overcome by packing the sole plate.
- *Poorly erected wall panels* – if not erected vertically, an uneven cavity can result, allowing the possibility of rain penetration. Breather paper should have been fixed with generous laps.

- *Missing cavity barriers* – good supervision is essential to ensure that cavity barriers (required for fire resistance) are not omitted, as their absence is almost impossible to detect.
- *Inadequate protection* – incomplete treatment of the timbers, usually as a result of poor quality control measures, increases the risk of rot. Inadequate weather protection can result in distortion as the frame dries.
  (Marshall *et al.*, 2003, pp 293–305).

It will be realised that few of these potential defects can be adequately checked during a superficial inspection, but problems that result from these defects may be detectable. There have also been a number of high-profile problems resulting from failure to tie the brick cladding adequately to the frame, and so evidence of bulging or non-vertical brickwork should be looked for when surveying timber-framed buildings.

The most common system-built houses were the Airey type (easily recognised by its 'shiplap' concrete cladding) and steel-framed houses, but well over 30 types were built throughout the UK. Following an investigation by the BRE in the early 1980s of a fire in an Airey house, some 24 systems were designated by the Housing Defects Act 1984 as being eligible for grants to carry out remedial works (often involving complete replacement of the external walls with traditional construction). Steel-framed houses were never grant aided, and no further grants are available for any remaining system houses.

```
                    ┌─────────────────────┐
────────────────────┤      S U M M A R Y      ├────────────────────
                    └─────────────────────┘

  • While the main points discussed in this section are less likely to give rise
    to negligence claims than the points discussed in the two preceding
    sections, they still require thorough inspection.
  • External joinery should be checked for rot, corrosion and security
    arrangements, and double glazed sealed units checked for condensation.
  • Internal partitions should be inspected for signs of structural movement
    and decorative condition, and sound insulation should be considered
    where very lightweight partitions are present.
  • Ventilation of suspended timber ground floors should be checked and
    the springiness of all timber floors should be tested.
  • Solid ground floors should be checked for signs of movement and
    dampness.
  • The type and estimated age of ceilings should be ascertained.
  • Internal joinery, chimney stacks and chimney breasts should be reported
    on.
  • Externally, the locality, the site, boundaries and permanent outbuildings
    should all be inspected.
  • Buildings of non-standard construction should always be considered
    carefully as many are not considered appropriate security for lending
    purposes.
```

Section 10
How to write the report

In this Section:

- *Importance of the report*
- *Writing style*
- *Reporting defects*
- *Other considerations*
- *Typical headings*

Importance of the report

So far, the surveyor has taken great care to ensure that the client's conditions of engagement have been confirmed, that the necessary surveying equipment has been assembled and that a detailed inspection has been planned and executed. However, all of this effort will have been completely wasted if the surveyor fails to write an acceptable report. The service the surveyor provides will be entirely judged on the contents of the report. It will therefore be realised that report writing is an extremely important skill for the surveyor to acquire – in fact, it is absolutely vital that this skill is developed before the surveyor ever reports to a client about the condition of a building.

Trainee surveyors in surveying practices have traditionally developed their report writing skills by reading other surveyors' reports, and by inspecting a building at the same time as an experienced surveyor, writing a 'shadow' report and comparing this with the actual report prepared by the experienced surveyor. It is only by serving this apprenticeship that the trainee can be sure to develop the essential skills before carrying out their first survey for a client. The trainee is, of course, likely to have studied report writing as part of their built environment degree course, but this does not by itself adequately prepare the surveyor for the real world. Many architects who carry out condition inspections have less experienced colleagues to assist them, and in this way the trainee is able to build up valuable experience.

The surveying practice will also wish its new surveyor to comply with its corporate report writing style, and although some firms allow some scope for individualism in report writing, many other firms use libraries of standard phrases so that all reports comply with the corporate style. It goes without saying that a firm's quality assurance procedures will require that the first few reports prepared by a new surveyor are very carefully checked by a supervising surveyor (who will also have inspected some of the properties). The lack of adequate supervision of inexperienced surveyors has been identified as one of the principal causes of professional indemnity insurance claims against surveying firms. It has been suggested that this careful 'minding' of junior members of any professional practice is an essential facet of true professionalism (Maister, 1997).

"lack of adequate supervision of junior staff is one of the principal causes of PI insurance claims against surveying firms"

Writing style

Obviously, clients will not tolerate poor grammar and spelling in their reports, and reports should be written in the third person (avoiding such words as 'I' and 'my'). Although most survey reports will contain some technical detail, it should be assumed that the client has no prior technical knowledge. It is thus necessary to explain technical terms where these cannot be avoided. Therefore, instead of simply referring to the 'wall dpc', a phrase such as 'the wall damp-proof course, which is a horizontal layer of impervious material, provided at low level in masonry walls and designed to prevent moisture rising from the ground to the interior' should be used in the first instance. Similarly, when referring to a rafter, it should be explained that this is 'an inclined roof timber', and so on. An alternative approach taken by some firms is to include in their survey reports a three-dimensional sketch of a building with the typical components annotated, rather than explaining what each component is and does in the text of the reports.

As indicated above, each surveying firm is likely to have its own style of report, and surveyors will probably be encouraged (or indeed required) to adopt standard paragraphs or phrases. There are commercially available as whole libraries of terminology – surveyors using these systems merely select the appropriate clauses when writing the report. Indeed, the individual drafting of a report to suit a particular property is now quite rare. Even if a surveyor does not formally adopt such a method of report writing, they will soon find they are using similar sentences repeatedly when drafting reports.

"individual drafting of a report is now quite rare"

While such practices certainly have their place in a highly competitive marketplace, it is important to be aware of possible drawbacks of such systems. First, each property is individual and no two buildings are identical. Therefore, there will always be some aspects of a survey report that are specific to that particular property and which will require individual drafting. Second, it is tempting to believe that because a report is largely compiled from tried and tested phrases it is not necessary to proofread it as carefully as if it had been individually drafted. This view is extremely dangerous and such reports require to be proofread with equal care.

Reporting defects

Guidance on site note-taking was offered in Section 6, and very similar advice is applicable here. For each element of construction it is necessary to report the following:

See also: What should be recorded?, page 47; How should the information be recorded?, page 47

1 Design and construction
2 Condition
3 Cause of any defects (or recommend further investigation)
4 Remedial work required

In addition, a legal judgement has suggested that for each particular defect the surveyor should advise on the following points:

1 Worst case and ultimate risk
2 Extent of work necessary
3 Complexity of work
4 Expense of work
5 The surveyor's opinion of what is happening

Advising on the cost of remedial work is, of course, fraught with difficulty. Say, for example, that the surveyor was to advise that a roof covering is likely to cost

£5,000 to replace and the lowest quotation the client could obtain after purchasing the property is double that amount then one would expect a claim to be forthcoming. When advising on the cost of work the surveyor should, wherever possible, obtain quotations from contractors, or where this is impossible, advise the client to do so before entering into a legal commitment to purchase or rent the property.

Typically, when inspecting any building the actual proportion of the structure and fabric that can be viewed is quite small – around 10 per cent. However, the surveyor is expected to use their knowledge of construction technology and their previous experience to alert the client to possible dangers. Thus, if there is no sub-floor ventilation at ground floor level and high moisture meter readings are obtained in the adjacent walls, the surveyor would be negligent not to advise a more detailed inspection of the floor to check for possible dry rot problems. Thus, the surveyor must give advice on areas that cannot be viewed where the evidence suggests that there may be a problem.

When reporting on defects, any observed defects should be placed in context – that is, the client should be advised whether a particular defect is usual or unusual in a particular type or age of property. If every house in a 1930s seaside suburb is likely to be suffering from cavity wall tie problems then the client should be advised of this fact. Following this advice, if the client is prepared to have the necessary remedial work carried out then they will purchase the

"any observed defects should be placed in context"

property, if not then they will look elsewhere. Such an approach should ensure that clients are not discouraged from purchasing a building just because it has defects. The important thing is that they purchase with a full appreciation of the condition and the work required to remedy the defects. This point is relevant to what the author has previously termed the 'surveyor's ethical dilemma' (Hoxley, 1995). As indicated in Section 3, most survey instructions result from recommendation or referral from a third party – usually another professional (normally a solicitor or estate agent), but sometimes a satisfied client. If every client is discouraged from purchasing each property surveyed, then these sources of new instructions will rapidly dry up. Thus, if defects are found, these should be placed in their correct context so that the client is not warned off purchasing a property just because it has similar defects to every other property in a particular locality.

See also: Taking instructions, page 17

Using the wall tie corrosion example given above, following the discovery of regular horizontal cracking in the external walls one of the surveyor's recommendations would be to arrange for a specialist to inspect the cavities with an endoscope. Such advice would be quite acceptable (although, as reported in Section 5, some 23 per cent of surveyors in a relatively recent research project indicated that 'they generally or occasionally' use an endoscope). However, as discussed in Section 4, care must be taken in recommending further investigation by specialists. The surveyor needs to aim for a balance between the cost to client and surveyor's liability, and should not recommend further investigation for work that they are capable of doing and/or should have already done.

*See also:
Investigating
practice, page
40;
Engagement
of specialists,
page 33*

Other considerations

Verbal reports should be avoided unless they are complete and the client should be advised to read the full written report before entering into any legal obligation. In today's busy world, it is common practice for people to read only the summary of a report. Therefore, the summary must be complete, and it should not introduce any material not included in the main body of the report. The author has adopted a method of making a list of the main points of a report as he dictates or types it. The drafting of the summary is therefore relatively easy once the report is complete. An alternative method is to delay drafting the summary section until the main body of the report has been proofread. The disadvantage of this method is that the client may contact the surveyor before the summary is written, which will make it difficult to provide a complete verbal report. It is for this reason that the author always prefers to draft the full report as soon as possible after the inspection.

The surveyor's professional indemnity insurer will usually insist that report summaries contain a standard limitation clause. Therefore, it is common for the final sentence in a summary to read, for example, 'We have not inspected covered, unexposed or inaccessible parts and are unable to say that any such parts are free from defect'. While limitation clauses are legal, their use is severely restricted by the Unfair Contract Terms Act 1977 and the Unfair Terms in Consumer Contracts Regulations 1994, and each allegation of negligence would be considered on its merits. Thus in the possible floor dry rot example used above, it is likely that reliance on this particular clause would fail. If,

"While limitation clauses are legal, their use is severely restricted"

however, asbestos was later discovered in an area to which the surveyor could not possibly have gained access, and there were no other reasons for the surveyor to suspect that asbestos had been used, then this clause might well succeed. Limitation clauses need to be included in the original conditions of engagement to be enforceable. In drafting standard conditions of engagement, surveyors need to be aware of the Unfair Contract Terms Act and the 1994 Regulations. The latter require consumers to be given the opportunity to negotiate contract terms, which suggests that the client's explicit attention should be drawn to any limitation clause at the time of taking instructions.

In any claim for professional negligence that relied on a limitation clause, it would be up to the surveyor to convince the court that the clause was reasonable. The court would apply the principles laid down in *Smith v. Eric S Bush* (1990) AC 831, which are as follows:

- Were the parties of equal bargaining power? If they were, the requirement of reasonableness is more easily discharged than if they were not.
- How difficult is the task being undertaken to which the clause applies? If the task is very difficult or dangerous, there may be a high risk of failure, which would be a pointer to the requirement of reasonableness being satisfied.
- What are the practical consequences of the decision on the requirement of reasonableness? This involves the amount of money potentially at stake and the ability of the parties to bear the loss involved, which in turn raises the question of insurance.

Typical headings

When carrying out an intermediate level service, such as the Homebuyer's Report, the format of the report is standard and free text is entered under predetermined headings. When drafting a building survey report, the headings used are entirely at the discretion of the surveyor.

The headings used in the RICS Homebuyer Survey and Valuation are listed in Box 10.1.

After the main body of the report, the report is signed and dated. The 'Description of the Homebuyer Service' (the conditions of engagement) is then attached to the report.

BOX 10.1: *RICS Homebuyer's Report headings*

A	**Introduction**	The main conditions of engagement are referred to and the objectives of the report are stated. The only free text to be entered here is the surveyor's overall opinion of the property.
B	**The Property and Location**	
B1	The Property	Type and age, construction, accommodation are stated here.
B2	The Location	Brief details of the location are provided, including any adverse matters.
B3	Circumstances of Inspection	Weather conditions, details of any occupiers, whether the property was furnished, etc.
C	**The Building**	
C1	Movement	See Section 7
C2	Timber Defects	See Section 7
C3	Dampness	See Section 7
C4	Condensation and Insulation	See Section 8
C5	The Exterior	See Section 7
C6	The Interior	See Section 9
D	**The Services and Site**	
D1	The Services	See Section 8
D2	Drainage	See Section 8
D3	The Site	See Section 9
E	**Legal and Other Matters**	
E1	Tenure	Whether freehold or leasehold, rents, service charges, etc. payable.
E2	Regulations, etc.	Any statutory matters such as listed status, contravention of Building Regulations, etc.
E3	Guarantees, etc.	Timber treatment, DPC, etc.
E4	Other Matters	Any other matters which need to be brought to the attention of the client's legal advisers.
F	**Summary**	
F1	Action	Urgent repairs, any specialist reports or quotations to be obtained prior to purchase.
F2	Maintenance Considerations	Any less serious matters which will require expenditure in the future.
F3	Other Considerations	Any other matter to be reported to client.
G	**Valuation**	
G1	Open Market Value	Value in present condition.
G2	Insurance Cover	Reinstatement value and gross external floor area.

Typical headings for a building survey and the main information conveyed in each section are indicated in Box 10.2 (as suggested in Section 6, this list could usefully form the basis of a checklist of the information to be recorded during the inspection). The report is then signed and dated.

See also: How should the information be recorded?, page 47

If the surveyor's detailed inspection is reflected in a carefully written and adequately proofread report then the client should receive an excellent service. But, it should be remembered that the best inspection will be of little worth without a well-drafted report.

BOX 10.2: *Building survey report headings*

Instructions	The name of the client and the date of signed acceptance of written conditions of engagement. The date(s) of inspection, the weather conditions, details of occupation, whether property was furnished and/or carpeted.
Situation	Orientation, approximate dimensions to any adjacent road junctions, nature of area, land use in immediate vicinity, street lighting, any restrictions on parking.
Description and Accommodation	Type and age of property. Overall plot size and brief description of accommodation and outbuildings. Details of tenure.
Site and Boundaries	Description of site, approximate guide of levels of garden, description and condition of boundaries and liability for upkeep if ascertained.
Roofs	Design in sufficient detail to enable the reader to be able to visualise the roof layout, details of all coverings, estimated age of covering, details of condition, estimated life remaining, any remedial work required.
Rainwater Goods	Materials, ages, condition, including evidence of any leaks or reverse falls. Details of discharge into drains – separate or combined, soakaways. Any remedial works required.
Roof Space	Access points, roof construction, evidence of any rot or insect infestation, slopes felted/boarded, evidence of any leaks, condition of party/gable walls, insulation, any water tanks and condition.

Chimney Stacks Numbers and locations, number of flues, materials including flashings, condition in roof spaces, presence of chimney breasts and if not how supported, flues in use, ventilation of redundant flues, condition of used flues including presence of linings.

External Walls Construction, materials, wall thicknesses, solid or cavity, condition, any evidence of movement, causes, assessment of age of movement, likelihood of continuing movement, DPC, any high moisture meter readings, sub-floor ventilation.

External Joinery Materials, design, condition, next redecoration required, any evidence of rot to timber joinery. Include windows, doors, any weatherboarding, roof fascia and barge boards.

Internal Doors Type, materials, condition, any requirements for fire doors, any remedial works required. Condition of ironmongery.

Internal Walls Loadbearing, non-loadbearing, condition, any evidence of movement, decorative condition.

Floors Solid or suspended timber, concrete, DPM, boarding, extent of any fitted coverings, deflection evident, adequacy of sub-floor ventilation, any evidence of rot or insect infestation, remedial works required.

Ceilings Type, condition of upper surfaces (in roof space and by raising floor boards), age, estimated life, decorative condition, remedial works required.

Staircases Type, materials, balustrades and handrails, any problems with design or headroom, condition, remedial works required.

Fire Insurance Gross external floor area, reinstatement value.

Services Types and ages, materials used, estimated lives, extent of any testing carried out or required, remedial works required. Include water, electricity, gas and drainage.

Sanitary Fittings Types, materials, ages and condition, including expected lives. Include bathroom, WC, utility room and kitchen fittings.

Outbuildings General comment on overall condition, including any major defects.

Summary (and Valuation) Complete but concise list of all work required and general comment on overall condition. Open market valuation in present condition if required. Any standard limitation clause required by insurers.

SUMMARY

- The report is what the entire service provided by the surveyor will be judged on.
- The report should be written in professional language, in the third person and assuming no prior knowledge on the part of the reader, who will frequently be a lay-person.
- Information technology may have taken much of the hard work out of drafting reports, but it is still essential that they are carefully proofread.
- For each element of construction, the report should consider:
  - design and construction
  - condition
  - cause of defects (or recommended further investigation) and
  - remedial work required.
- Defects should be placed in context, both geographically and historically.
- When providing estimates of remedial works it is important to emphasise that these are given as a guide only and to recommend that quotations be obtained from builders before entering into a legally binding contact to purchase or lease the building.
- Summaries should be provided to reports and these must be complete.
- It is not possible to exclude liability, but it is possible to include limitation clauses, provided they are reasonable. Professional indemnity insurers will have a view on the wording of such clauses, which must also be agreed between the surveyor and the client at the outset.

Section 11
Case study – building survey report

Case study building

Just as in life, we learn best from our mistakes – so when undertaking surveys, the most enduring lessons are those provided by our errors. Hopefully, these will not be too expensive for the new surveyor or their firm, but in an increasingly litigious society even the smallest error seems to have the habit of developing into an expensive claim. What is certain is that no surveyor is ever likely to progress through their career in the modern world without facing a claim for professional negligence. Hopefully, by adopting a thoroughly professional approach in preparing for the survey, inspecting the building and writing the report, such claims will be few and far between.

The presentation of an excellent example of a building survey report in this final section was considered, but instead it was decided that far more would be learned from the analysis of a rather poor report. However, this report is not a work of fiction, but an actual survey report carried out by an experienced surveyor. In fact, the survey is an early example of a seller's report as it was commissioned by the agents engaged to dispose of the property by auction. The report was given to all parties viewing the property before the auction. Obviously, the names of the surveyor and the property and location details have been amended so that complete anonymity is respected. Apart from these changes, the report is reproduced exactly as it was produced, warts and all, and there are plenty of these. At least 20 spelling or grammatical errors have been identified. As will be seen from the penultimate paragraph of the report, the surveyor has sought to excuse these deficiencies in presentation on the grounds of having to provide the report at short notice!

The commentary is based on an inspection after the survey was carried out. It is recommended that the report be read initially without reading the commentary. This will enable the reader to then compare his or her own views with the commentary when undertaking a second reading.

Overall, the surveyor's opinion – that the property is structurally sound but requires extensive modernisation, and will provide a new owner with the opportunity to restore it without having to undo the work of others – is a valid one. However, there are a number of problem areas, where the surveyor has left himself vulnerable to potential claims.

Ambridge Hall is a seven-bedroom, two-storey house constructed in the Georgian style about 200 years ago and having a separate staff flat at ground floor level. The house is located in a rural position and occupies a plot of approximately 3 hectares. The report of Joseph Grundy follows (comments are contained in the italic formatted bullet points at the end of each section).

Building Survey of Ambridge Hall, Ambridge, Borsetshire

Location and Description

The property comprises a detached country house dating from the late 18th century and approximately 200 years old.

The construction is conventional in solid brick elevations under pitched and tiled roofs with solid and suspended timber floors. The main structure which is approximately square has two storeys; the extension containing part of the self-contained flat is single storey with a single slope lean-to roof.

The house faces east and is constructed on a more or less level site in a semi-rural location between the villages of Ambridge and Darrington. It is located some 4 or 5 miles to the north-east of Borchester.

The survey relates to the house and immediate outbuildings only. No inspection of the gardens or land being sold with the house has been made.

It is understood that the property is listed Grade II as of architectural and historic interest. Close to the house stands a former Coach house now utilised as garages and stores and also further storage buildings constructed of brick under a single slope slate roof. There is also an area of walled garden to the west of the house.

- *There is some tautology in the first paragraph as it is not necessary to give both of these figures.*
- *There is nothing to say WHEN the inspection was carried out or what the weather conditions were at the time. In view of comments made later about the watertightness of the rainwater goods, the client would be entitled to believe that there was heavy rainfall at the time of the inspection.*
- *There is no mention of who the client is or how the conditions of engagement have been confirmed. (Fellow Archers fans may suspend disbelief a little longer by assuming that the clients are a Mr and Mrs R. Snell!)*
- *The distance from Borchester is rather imprecise. The surveyor should have checked his car mileage from the office.*

- *The surveyor has advised the client that the property is Grade II listed, but nowhere in the report have the full financial implications of this fact been emphasised.*

Accommodation

The accommodation is as follows:

On the ground floor:
> Entrance hall; Dining room; Staircase Hall; Cellar; Drawing room, Sitting room; Rear hall; Cloakroom; Staff sitting room; Butler's pantry; Kitchen.

Separate self contained flat:
> Sitting room; Inner corridor; Utility room; Kitchen.

On the first floor:
> 7 Bedrooms; 2 Bathrooms; Separate W.C.

- *There is probably sufficient detail in this description of the accommodation, but there in no way that the client is able to identify which bedroom is which. Some further detail to orientate each bedroom (and to distinguish between the bathrooms) would have been useful.*
- *No details have been provided anywhere in the report about the plot size, site and boundaries or tenure. The flat was tenanted at the time of the author's inspection.*

Construction and State of Repair

The Roofs

The house has a pitched and hipped timber framed roof covered with black glazed pantiles. There is a central flat section with a lantern roof light located above the stairwell and this flat section is covered with bituminous felt. Black glazed pantiles cover the roof slopes including the single slope roof above the single storey rear extension.

It is apparent that the roof coverings have been relaid comparatively recently, probably in the last 2 or 3 years. Roof slopes are even with no signs of any undue deflection or sagging. The black pantiles are mostly the traditional glazed variety, but to some of the inner slopes there are low grade tar-dipped pantiles in evidence.

The pantiles are generally in satisfactory condition and show no signs of any serious decay or failure. Details include tile and cement ridges and hips, and lead valleys and flashings and these are generally sound and sufficient.

The flat section of roof is covered with bituminous felt that was renewed very recently. The felt is in satisfactory condition and shows no signs of any deterioration. The fall of this roof is to the guttering at the rear. No inspection of the roof light could be made from the exterior. The internal appearance of the timbers is poor and it may be found that some attention is required externally when access is gained to the roof top.

There are four chimney stacks built of brick and mortar. These are more or less square and upright and in fair structural order. Brick and mortar materials have been the subject of repairs in recent years and currently they are in reasonable condition. Flashings are in lead and felt and these are in fair condition, although some moisture penetration to the interior is apparent and this may well require some further attention in the years to come.

The roof framework is approached via access hatches above two of the upper bedrooms. The framework is in original softwood timbers with principal and common rafters, purlins and collars. There has been some recent minor repairs and reinforcements of the framework.

Roof timbers are affected by active woodworm infestation and this will require spray treatment which works should be undertaken by a reputible company with a guarantee provided. Otherwise the timbers are sound and sufficient with no signs of any outbreaks of rot and decay and with moisture content levels within an acceptable range.

The roof is felted beneath the tiles and there was no sign of any water penetration into the interior. However, the void area has not been provided with adequate insulation and this work will have to be put in hand.

The single storey extension is provided with a roof framework in softwood timbers that are of a similar age to that of the main roof structure.

Timbers are again affected by active woodworm infestation and spray treatment works are required.

- *Again, there is some repetition in the first paragraph of this section, with 'black glazed pantiles' mentioned twice. This suggests inadequate proofreading.*
- *There is some inconsistency in reporting in that the surveyor says he has not been able to inspect the roof-light and yet he reports on the condition of the bituminous felt covered roof, at the centre of which is the roof-light. Is it possible that the surveyor has in fact not inspected this central area, but has accepted someone's assurance that the felt covering has been renewed very recently? There is no comment about the limited life of bituminous felt coverings to flat roofs.*
- *In the paragraph about the chimney stacks, nothing is said about the limited life of felt flashings (these are where the stacks abut the flat roof, and should ideally have lead flashings over them).*
- *There is nothing that most clients take more exception to than dampness problems, and the casual way in which the damp penetration around the chimney stacks is reported is very poor. To suggest that this problem 'may require some further attention in the years to come' considerably understates both the problem and the extensive further investigation work required to discover the actual cause of the problem before any remedial work can be put in hand.*
- *Again, the description of the roof construction lacks detail, and technical terms are used without any explanation of what they refer to.*
- *Reading the final paragraph of this section it is not clear whether the single-storey roof void has any insulation and the client would be quite entitled to assume that insulation existed (it did not).*

Gutters and Pipes

Gutters were entirely renewed 2 or 3 years ago in upvc materials, and these connect to both upvc and older cast iron down pipes and hopperheads. These in turn connect to trapped gulleys formed of brick and concrete and then to underground soakaways.

Materials are of adequate size and capacity to cope with normal levels of discharge. There was no sign of any leakages to the system at the time of inspection nor is there any evidence of any weeping of joints. Hopperheads require clearing of some debris as do trapped gulleys, which work will have to be carried out on a regular basis.

Cast iron materials show some minor signs of corrosion beneath the decorations. Some attention to these will be necessary in the years to come. There was no obvious above ground signs to suggest any failure of the underground drains or soakaways.

- *In this section, a clear statement is made that there is no sign of any leaks from the rainwater goods. Since there is no statement about the weather conditions at the time of the inspection, we are entitled to assume that it was raining. Presumably, the surveyor was not surprised to receive a telephone call from his clients the first time it rained after they took up occupation!*
- *It is not clear what 'obvious above ground signs' there would be to suggest failure of the underground drains or soakaways. This comment is super-fluous and leaves the surveyor open to criticism.*

The Elevations
The main elevations are constructed of solid 13″ and 9″ red brick with lime-stone windowcills, rubbed and guaged red brick arches and penny rounded (i.e. the joints are struck with a straight line) mortar pointing.

The walls are upright with no signs of any significant deflection or leaning. There is some evidence of minor settlement that has occurred over the years as indicated by one or two small cracks in the brickwork here and there, for example between the main structure and the rear extension where the brickwork between one and the other has not been keyed in. The movement is of a minor nature, appears to have stabilised and is considered unlikely to continue to any significant extent in normal climatic conditions. The bricks and mortar are genereally in reasonable condition for their age. A number of the bricks are becoming badly spalled however and this is most noticeable at the base of the walls particularly to the east (front) and south elevations. In the years to come it will be necessary to repair the bricks by patching in matching replacement units where the existing are badly weathered.

The bricks are of an age where they have become rather porous and are prone to allowing moisture to penetrate. Some damp penetration was apparent in one or two of the upper rooms. This is a typical problem to be overcome in properties of this type and age. Improved ventilation and heating of the house may assist in this regard and it is advised that the damp penetration is monitored for a while before any decisions are made as to repairs.

The mortar pointing is generally in reasonable condition for its age. Some patch repairs have been carried out here and there in a hard cement based mortar which is proving more damaging than beneficial. It is advised that in the years to come this work is renewed with a soft lime based mortar which will not cause excessive weathering of the brick surfaces. In the years to come some judicious and sympathetic renewal of the mortar pointing may become desirable although such work should only be undertaken by skilled labour.

The cellar retaining walls and floors are formed of brick and concrete which exhibit some signs of moisture penetration and dampness. This is to some extent to be expected and in this instance is not considered particularly serious. Again some patch repairs to the brickwork and concrete may be found necessary in the years to come in order to preserve the brickwork and minimise the possibility of structural failure.

- *Again, the way in which the cracking in the brickwork of the external walls is reported is far too casual – 'one or two small cracks in the brickwork here and there'. It is to be hoped that for his own sake the surveyor has taken much more detailed notes of the cracking, supported where necessary by sketches, than he has reported to the client.*
- *The surveyor has failed to diagnose that spalling at the lower levels of the external walls is the result of the lack of a damp-proof course and subsequent frost action.*
- *Reading between the lines of the third paragraph of this section, the surveyor seems to be in two minds as to the cause of the dampness at first floor level. He suggests initially that it is due to penetrating dampness, but his subsequent comment about improved ventilation and heating leads one to suspect that he thinks that condensation may be the cause.*

> *No one, least of all the client, should have to read between the lines of any part of the report – it should be explicit. The second inspection suggested that the problem was predominantly one of condensation – the dampness was restricted to the north-facing bedrooms.*
> - *The comments about a softer lime mortar for repointing are good, but again there is some repetition in this section.*
> - *Has any thought been given to dehumidifying mechanical ventilation of the cellar?*

Damp Proofing

Tests were conducted with an electronic damp meter around the house. Rising dampness was detected in most of the rooms, although in the drawing and sitting rooms dry lining is provided which is preventing any damage to interior finishes.

It is now advised that the property is provided with an injected chemical damp proof course throughout. This work should again be undertaken by a reputible company and a guarantee provided.

> - *Apart from not being able to spell 'reputable', the advice about installing a damp-proof course is probably correct. However, there is no mention of the need for replastering or replacement of dry linings. The client would be entitled to feel very aggrieved on discovering that this additional work was necessary and might well seek recompense from the surveyor.*

Floors

At ground level there are suspended timber floors in the dining room, drawing room, sitting room and in walk-in pantry.

Elsewhere there are solid concrete floors with a rather cracked stone flag finish in the entrance hall and with a quarry tile finish to the inner hall.

The suspended timber floors are not provided with any sub floor ventilation at all, although the cellar lies partly beneath the sitting room where ventilation is improved.

Moisture content in the floorboards was found to be in the high range and given the absence of sub floor ventilation it is likely that outbreaks of woodworm exists beneath the floors and it is possible that some outbreaks of rot and decay are occurring in joist ends. There appears to be no wholesale failure of the floors to date and if any remedial works are found to be necessary these are likely to be repairs rather than wholesale renewal. In addition it is advised that an adequate number of airbricks are provided in the foot of the walls where there are suspended timber floors.

The flag stone and quarry tile floors are uneven and cracked with age and are affected by some levels of dampness. If required they can continue in use as existing, although any covering of these floors with carpeting is likely to lead to an unacceptable build up of moisture. The concrete floors in the kitchen and in the rear self-contained flat are in such poor condition as will necessitate total renewal.

To the upper storey the suspended timber floors are partly visible and are in softwood with boards running largely from front to back and with joists from side to side. In some of the rooms there is fitted carpet throughout and a thorough inspection was possible only in isolated areas. Joists are exposed in one or two places only.

The floorboards and sub floor joists at first floor level are affected by active woodworm infestation and spray treatment works are now required. There were no outbreaks of rot and decay apparent, although the flooring will be at risk in places where dampness has entered into the structure, for example from porous 18th century brickwork and poor chute work in gutters and pipes. One suspect area of this kind is to the floorboards adjacent to the damp reveals inside the separate W.C. at first floor level, and also to the joists in the vicinity of the washbasin in bedroom 7 where damp penetration from the external brickwork is particularly in evidence. These areas should be exposed for further inspection when it is possible to do so.

Part leakage or failure of plumbing and sanitary appliances may also be a cause for decay in floor timbers. Again it is impossible to know the extent of such problems in areas of the bathrooms and W.C. and this will only become evident when it is possible to fully expose the floors.

- *The advice about the lack of sub-floor ventilation and the need to provide it is appropriate, but the dangers of possible dry rot attack and the need for further investigation should have been made much more explicit. The surveyor does not indicate whether he has raised any floorboards – he certainly should have done so as part of a full building survey.*

- *The comment 'there appears to be no wholesale failure of the floors to date' seems certain to fill the client with confidence! There are very few instances in which the word 'appears' would be appropriate in a survey report. Either something is or it isn't. To use the words 'appears' or 'seems' is invariably to suggest that the surveyor lacks confidence in his opinions or advice.*

- *Again, the surveyor's failure to be explicit about which floors are covered is a serious failing. He will not be able to rely on lack of access to raise floorboards unless he says which floors he has not been able to inspect in detail.*

- *The term 'poor chute work in gutters and pipes' is rather antiquated and is at odds with the comments made by the surveyor under the heading 'Gutters and Pipes'.*

- *Based on the second inspection, it is believed that the damp flooring in the separate WC and bedroom 7 has far more to do with leaking plumbing and sanitary fittings than with dampness penetrating through the walls. The surveyor also seems to have come to this conclusion rather late, judging from the final paragraph of this section. However, the reader is left wondering just what is the cause of this problem.*

Joinery

Windows throughout the house are of the vertical sliding sash type, double hung in box frames. These have been fairly well maintained over the years although some further repairs are now required. There are some fixed opening lights which require easing and adjusting, for example to the entrance. Also in bedroom 1 there are broken sash cords. In addition one or two of the glazing panes are cracked, for example in the dining room. The timber sill to the main bathroom window is rotted and in need of repair. Given these repairs and regular maintenance the sash windows should continue to function adequately for a fair number of years to come. Other external joinery comprises the lantern light above the stairwell, the panel and glazed front door with classical timber surrounds. In addition there are timber and glazed rear doors. The lantern has been referred to earlier in the report. The doors and timber surrounds to the front door are generally in reasonable condition with no signs of any serious failures.

Internal joinery comprises two staircases, timber panel doors with softwood architraves and skirting boards, a variety of fitted and built-in cupboards and the kitchen and utility fittings. This is mostly original and of reasonable quality. Some of the doors are now slightly misshapen by slight structural settlement and/or deflection of floors which has occurred over many years. This is to some extent a normal problem to be overcome in this type of property.

Joinery is affected by wear and tear, but there were no signs of any outbreaks of rot or decay where I was able to inspect. Please note it was not possible to lift skirtings etc. to view the undersides. Given some minor repairs and reinstatement the existing joinery should continue to function adequately for a fair number of years to come. The joinery is included in the listing of the house and any alteration or removal of it will require listed building consent.

- *Some sensible advice is given in this section, but the surveyor has not made the fact explicit that because of the listed status of the building any new owner would not be able to install replacement uPVC windows.*
- *For the first time, a personal pronoun ('I') has crept into the report.*

Plasterwork and Partitions
Ceilings throughout the house appear to be entirely the original of early lathe and plaster construction. These are cracked and in some places sagging slightly with age. One section in the staff sitting room has failed and has been cleared away ready for repair. Elsewhere the ceilings to the upper landing and in bedroom 1 are badly cracked. That in bedroom 4 as been overlaid with plasterboard leaving little of the ornamental cornice on view.

In terms of the character of the property it is desirable that these ceilings are repaired rather than renewed with plasterboard. They are quite capable of repair. Repairs should be carried out where the ceilings are starting to fail and are sagging and where they are badly cracked. Again such work should be undertaken by skilled labour.

Internal partitions are formed of both brick and timber stud and plaster. These are more or less straight and upright and show no signs of any structural movement or failure. Internal plastered finishes are again very old and mostly original. Some damage to the plasterwork has occurred where dampness has entered into the structure, for example to the upper landing and in some of the bedrooms where penetrating dampness is apparent. Patch repair of the plasterwork will again be necessary.

- *No comment, apart from the fact that presumably the ceilings are of 'lath' and plaster.*

Decorations
Internally the house is in need of total redecoration. Externally the paint-work is in fair condition but in places is starting to become worn and peeling to some of the surfaces and renewal will be necessary in the next year or two. In the meantime some touching in may become necessary to areas where paint is peeling badly in order to protect the timbers beneath.

- *It is unusual to combine internal and external decorations in one section like this. The external decorative condition is best dealt with when reporting on the exterior.*

Sanitation and Services

Drainage
Foul waste drains from the property by means of 4.5″ cast iron soil pipes on the flank and rear elevations. This connects to an underground drain that runs beneath the rear of the property and to a septic tank behind the stable block on the north side. The drains are 6″ diameter in glazed clay. They are badly silted and affected by root penetration and undoubtedly subject to leakage. The tank is very old and one of its chambers could not be reached. It is apparent that the tank is in working order. Its brick and concrete construction is showing signs of deterioration and will require renewal in the course of the next few years. It is advised that the work should be put in hand in the context of any major renovation of the property.

- *The surveyor has said that the drains are undoubtedly leaking, but he has said absolutely nothing about replacing them! The client will assume that it is acceptable to do nothing about these leaks.*

- *Although the surveyor has offered the sensible advice that the septic tank is likely to require renewal in the next few years, he has said that it is in working order. It is impossible to give this advice based on a simple inspection at one point in time. If the clients were to discover that after one week of using a washing machine twice a day and a dishwasher once a day the tank is unable to cope then it is going to need replacing very much sooner than advised by the surveyor, who do you think is likely to be paying for the replacement?*

Water Supply

Water is supplied to the premises from a main located beneath a cover in the tin shed outside the backdoor of the house. Water is pumped to the property at present. Mains water is available from the nearby road and could be connected to the property without too much inconvenience. If it is intended to continue with the existing supply adequacy of the well and pumping machinery should be established as should the quality of the water.

- *Due to what is probably a typing error, this entire paragraph is extremely confusing. What the surveyor should have said is that there is a well (not a main) in the tin shed. A first reading suggests that mains water is connected, and again because of failure to proofread this report adequately it is possible that the surveyor and his insurers will be paying for this mains supply to be connected.*
- *The property is surrounded by arable farmland and therefore checking the quality of the water for nitrates and other chemicals will be a high priority.*

Hot and Cold Water Services

Hot and cold water services are provided around the house in a mixture of lead, cast iron and copper pipework. Some of this is run externally and will be prone to frost damage. One of the cold water systems is galvanised metal and is unhygenic. The hot water system is awkwardly located in the kitchen. It is advised that in the context of modernisation and improvement of the property that hot and cold water service installations will have to be entirely renewed.

- *Careful proofreading would have led the surveyor to change 'system' to 'cistern' on the two occasions it appears in this paragraph (as well as hopefully to correct other spelling mistakes in the report – the typist has obviously not heard of a spell checker!).*

- *The need to replace the plumbing and tanks is clear, but the surveyor has not mentioned the health hazards of lead pipework.*

Sanitary Fittings

The present sanitary installations are old and it is assumed that all kitchens and bathrooms will be refitted in the course of refurbishment and updating.

- *Good advice, but we are never told anywhere in the report just what fittings currently exist.*

Electrical Installation

The electricity meters and switchgear are located in the ground floor flat. Electrical wiring in pvc is installed around the house and this is some 15–20 years old. The work was undertaken to a simple specification with a limited supply of light and socket fittings and much surface run ducting. We would advise that this be disregarded in your consideration of the purchase so that total rewiring of the building should be undertaken as part of overall refurbishment.

- *Good advice.*

Heating

There are fireplaces located in the main reception rooms and in some of the upper bedrooms where they have been covered. Where the flues could be inspected they were found to be in original brickwork. If it is intended that fireplaces should be put into regular use it will probably be necessary to introduce flue linings to the existing brick chimney flues. The remaining chimney breasts are structurally sound.

There is no central heating to the property although one or two old night storage heaters are apparent here and there. Otherwise there is a dependance on portable electric heaters.

- *The advice about lining flues to be used is correct, but ventilation of redundant flues should also have been recommended.*

- *The use of the term 'remaining chimney breasts' suggests that some may have been removed. If so, details of support should have been provided.*

The Outbuildings

The stable block is constructed of 9″ brick with a pitched and hipped timber framed roof covered with pantiles. The building is generally dilapidated with a missing window to one flank wall, failing plaster ceiling and walls to the attic room and woodworm in roof and floor timbers. Creeper growth is penetrating the roof in places which should of course be discouraged. Walls are affected by some moisture penetration and by rising dampness. External masonry would benefit from brick and mortar repairs.

The brick and slate range of outbuildings is in a poor state of repair with leaking and failing roofs that are overrun with creeper, old and dilapidated doors and joinery and spalled and porous brickwork. The range of timber and tin buildings is also dilapidated and is currently unsightly. The garden wall is overrun with creeper at one end where little could be seen. Elsewhere the tile coping is failing and in need of repair.

These are a number of trees growing close to the foundations of the house, notably the holly and oak at the north-east corner. These should be trimmed back or removed to prevent the possibility of root action from affecting foundations. There is also Virginia and other creeper on the house which should not be allowed to overrun and clog gutters etc.

- *The descriptions of the outbuildings and the comments about their overall condition are at about the correct level of detail.*
- *It is believed that there is a clay subsoil in the area in which the property is located. The advice about trimming or removal of vegetation may therefore be inappropriate as such work could lead to heave of the foundations.*

Conclusions

It will be apparent from the above report that while the property has some advantage in being largely unaltered from its original form, the extent of updating that is now required is considerable. Nevertheless the structure and fabric constitutes sufficient base for the necessary repairs and improvements although the costs involved are likely to be high. To properly repair the house and to update the service installations and to provide central heating and to under-take basic repairs to the outbuilding, we think it would be necessary to allow a budget cost of between £40,000–£45,000 to which VAT presently at 17.5% must be added. This approximate estimate would not include any updating of kitchen or bathroom fittings. Obviously any expenditure on refitting will depend upon the extent and quality of work required and there may well be some overlap with repair costs.

It is hoped that this report will provide sufficient information for your purposes. The report has been prepared at short notice and we apologise if any minor errors have crept in as a result.

This report should be read in conjunction with the Conditions of Engagement already notified to you.

JOSEPH GRUNDY

For RODWAY AND WATSON

SURVEYORS

BORCHESTER

[Date]

- *There is no summary of works required or any standard limitation clause.*
- *The estimated costs of the remedial work are on the low side.*

Concluding comments

In addition to the points identified in the above commentary, it will have been noted that the surveyor's use of English is rather poor. Some phrases are repeated several times – 'here and there' and 'more or less' seem to be great favourites. Another criticism is that there is a lack of both technical detail and precision throughout the report. Although verbosity is not to be encouraged, this report is far too short bearing in mind the size of the house. Had the headings recommended in this guide been adopted, it is likely that more detail would have been incorporated. The failure to identify exactly which floors were covered and exactly where the external wall cracking was, for example, may cause the surveyor problems in the event of a complaint or claim.

The author has no idea whether the eventual purchaser of the property relied on this survey report, but it will be seen from the discussion in this section that had he done so then the probability of a claim resulting would have been high. There is no guarantee that if a reader follows every piece of advice offered in this section and throughout this guide then they will not be sued. However, by following the advice given, the chances of such an unfortunate event will be greatly reduced.

References and further reading

Introductory

Hollis, M. (1995a). *Property Services, Part 1: The Aims of a Survey,* The Chartered Surveyors' Education Channel Video.

Hollis, M. (1995b). *Property Services, Part 2: The Exterior,* The Chartered Surveyors' Education Channel Video.

Hollis, M. (1995c). *Property Services, Part 3: The Interior,* The Chartered Surveyors' Education Channel Video.

Hollis, M. (1995d). *Property Services, Part 4: The Report,* The Chartered Surveyors' Education Channel Video.

Marshall, D., Worthing, D. and Heath, R. (2003). *Understanding Housing Defects,* Estates Gazette, London.

Marshall, D. and Worthing. D. (2006). *The Construction of Houses,* Estates Gazette, London.

Parnham, P. and Rispin, C. (2001). *Residential Property Appraisal,* Spon Press, London.

RICS (2004a). *Building Surveys of Residential Property,* RICS Guidance Note, The Royal Institution of Chartered Surveyors, London.

RICS (2005a). *Building Surveys and Inspections of Commercial and Industrial Property,* RICS Guidance Note, The Royal Institution of Chartered Surveyors, London.

RICS (2005b). *The RICS Homebuyer Survey and Valuation Service 2005,* RICS Practice Note, The Royal Institution of Chartered Surveyors, London.

Advanced

Bravery, A., Berry, R., Carey, J. and Cooper, D. (2003). *Recognising Wood Rot and Insect Damage in Buildings,* Building Research Establishment, Watford.

BRE (1995). *Assessment of Damage in Low-rise Buildings*, BRE Digest 251, Building Research Establishment, Watford.

BSI (2008). *British Standard 761, Requirements for Electrical Installations*, British Standards Institution, London.

CIC (1997). *Definitions of Inspections and Surveys of Buildings,* Construction Industry Council, London.

CIRIA (1986). *Report 111 Structural Renovation of Traditional Buildings*, Construction Industry Research and Information Association, London (reprinted 1994 with update amendments).

Coday, A. and Hoxley, M. (2001). 'The portable test equipment being used for commercial building surveys', *Structural Survey,* vol. 19, no. 4, pp 173–184.

Council of Mortgage Lenders (2008). *Lenders' Handbook*, online at: www.cml.org.uk/handbook.

Dixon, D. W. and Scivyer, C. (1999). 'Radon and remedial measures', *Structural Survey,* vol. 17, no. 3, pp 154–159.

Dunster, A. and Holton, I. (2000). 'Assessment of ageing high alumina cement concrete', *Structural Survey,* vol. 18, no. 1, pp 16–21.

Hoxley, M. (1995). 'How do clients select a surveyor?', *Structural Survey,* vol. 13, no. 2, pp 6–12.

HM Government (2006), *Sample Home Condition Report*, online at: www.homeinformationpacks.gov.uk/pdf/sampleHCR.pdf.

IStructE (2000). *Subsidence of Low Rise Buildings: A Guide for Professionals and Property Owners*, The Institution of Structural Engineers, London.

Maister, D. (1997). *True Professionalism: The Courage to Care About Your People, Your Clients, and Your Career,* The Free Press, New York.

Parnham, P. and Russen L. (2008). *Domestic Energy Assessors Handbook,* RICS Books, London.

Parrett, M. (2006). *Guide to Building Pathology: Litigation*, DVD, Limelite Media, London.

RICS (2004b). *Your Guide to Personal Safety at Work,* The Royal Institution of Chartered Surveyors, London.

Robson, P. (1999). *Structural Repair of Traditional Buildings,* Donhead Press, Donhead St Mary, Dorset.

Wilkin, D. and Baggott, R. (1994). 'Technical factors influencing decisions to select underpinning on shrinkable clay', *Structural Survey*, vol. 12, no. 2, pp 10–14.

Woodland Trust (2008). *Leaf Identification Swatch Book*, Woodland Trust, Grantham.

Index